D0497821

Current
CONTROVERSIES

The Abortion Controversy

Other books in the Current Controversies Series

The Abortion Controversy

Lucinda Almond, Book Editor

GREENHAVEN PRESS

An imprint of Thomson Gale, a part of The Thomson Corporation

Detroit • New York • San Francisco • New Haven, Conn. • Waterville, Maine • London

THOMSON

*

™

GALE

Christine Nasso, *Publisher*
Elizabeth Des Chenes, *Managing Editor*

© 2007 Thomson Gale, a part of The Thomson Corporation.

Thomson and Star logo are trademarks and Gale and Greenhaven Press are registered trademarks used herein under license.

For more information, contact:
Greenhaven Press
27500 Drake Rd.
Farmington Hills, MI 48331-3535
Or you can visit our Internet site at http://www.gale.com

Articles in Greenhaven Press anthologies are often edited for length to meet page requirements. In addition, original titles of these works are changed to clearly present the main thesis and to explicitly indicate the author's opinion. Every effort is made to ensure that Greenhaven Press accurately reflects the original intent of the authors. Every effort has been made to trace the owners of copyrighted material.

Cover photograph reproduced by permission of Greg Smith/Corbis.

LIBRARY OF CONGRESS CATALOGING-IN-PUBLICATION DATA

The abortion controversy / Lucinda Almond, book editor.
    p. cm. -- (Current controversies)
    Includes bibliographical references and index.
    ISBN-13: 978-0-7377-3273-3 (hardcover)
    ISBN-13: 978-0-7377-3274-0 (pbk.)
    1. Abortion--Moral and ethical aspects--Juvenile literature. I. Almond, Lucinda.
    HQ767.15.A274 2007
    363.46--dc22
                                                                    2007004509

ISBN-10: 0-7377-3273-3 (hardcover)
ISBN-10: 0-7377-3274-1 (pbk.)

Printed in the United States of America
10 9 8 7 6 5 4 3 2 1

Contents

Foreword

By definition, controversies are "discussions of questions in which opposing opinions clash" (Webster's Twentieth Century Dictionary Unabridged). Few would deny that controversies are a pervasive part of the human condition and exist on virtually every level of human enterprise. Controversies transpire between individuals and among groups, within nations and between nations. Controversies supply the grist necessary for progress by providing challenges and challengers to the status quo. They also create atmospheres where strife and warfare can flourish. A world without controversies would be a peaceful world; but it also would be, by and large, static and prosaic.

The Series' Purpose

The purpose of the Current Controversies series is to explore many of the social, political, and economic controversies dominating the national and international scenes today. Titles selected for inclusion in the series are highly focused and specific. For example, from the larger category of criminal justice, Current Controversies deals with specific topics such as police brutality, gun control, white collar crime, and others. The debates in Current Controversies also are presented in a useful, timeless fashion. Articles and book excerpts included in each title are selected if they contribute valuable, long-range ideas to the overall debate. And wherever possible, current information is enhanced with historical documents and other relevant materials. Thus, while individual titles are current in focus, every effort is made to ensure that they will not become quickly outdated. Books in the Current Controversies series will remain important resources for librarians, teachers, and students for many years.

In addition to keeping the titles focused and specific, great care is taken in the editorial format of each book in the series. Book introductions and chapter prefaces are offered to provide background material for readers. Chapters are organized around several key questions that are answered with diverse opinions representing all points on the political spectrum. Materials in each chapter include opinions in which authors clearly disagree as well as alternative opinions in which authors may agree on a broader issue but disagree on the possible solutions. In this way, the content of each volume in Current Controversies mirrors the mosaic of opinions encountered in society. Readers will quickly realize that there are many viable answers to these complex issues. By questioning each author's conclusions, students and casual readers can begin to develop the critical thinking skills so important to evaluating opinionated material.

Current Controversies is also ideal for controlled research. Each anthology in the series is composed of primary sources taken from a wide gamut of informational categories including periodicals, newspapers, books, U.S. and foreign government documents, and the publications of private and public organizations. Readers will find factual support for reports, debates, and research papers covering all areas of important issues. In addition, an annotated table of contents, an index, a book and periodical bibliography, and a list of organizations to contact are included in each book to expedite further research.

Perhaps more than ever before in history, people are confronted with diverse and contradictory information. During the Persian Gulf War, for example, the public was not only treated to minute-to-minute coverage of the war, it was also inundated with critiques of the coverage and countless analyses of the factors motivating U.S. involvement. Being able to sort through the plethora of opinions accompanying today's major issues, and to draw one's own conclusions, can be a complicated and frustrating struggle. It is the editors' hope that Current Controversies will help readers with this struggle.

Introduction

In the landmark case *Roe v. Wade* (1973) the U.S. Supreme Court ruled that women had the legal right to abortion. This decision was based on the Fourteenth Amendment that guarantees the right to privacy. The Court further determined that a woman's right to an abortion outweighed the rights of a nonviable fetus. The Court's ruling expressly prohibited interference by the states and ruled that states must allow late-term abortions, even if the fetus is viable, if the woman's life was in danger.

Since that ruling, an abortion debate has rocked the United States. Pro-choice and pro-life factions continue to clash in court, on the streets, and in the media. Protests, violence, and deaths are the result of many of these clashes as both sides struggle to gain prominence and effect legal changes that reflect their respective philosophies and beliefs.

Abortion rights advocates are deeply committed to a woman's right to choose and vehemently oppose any restrictions to abortion. They argue that a fetus is not a person and that some members of society who believe otherwise should not impose their beliefs on others. The impact of childbirth, both physically and financially, is so great that abortion proponents argue that women would lose control over their lives without reproductive rights. In the 1992 court case *Planned Parenthood v. Casey*, the U.S. Supreme Court acknowledged that "the ability of women to participate equally in the economic and social life of the nation has been facilitated by their ability to control their reproductive lives."

Pro-choice supporters argue that individuals, not religious leaders or the government, should decide when they have children. They believe that government-imposed religious belief–based laws have no place in a country founded by individuals who were escaping religious oppression. It is argued that some

churches refuse to give men and women any kind of reproductive choices, including birth control. Feminist Catholic Susan A. Farrel questions the justice of church policies that ban
contraception and concludes that such a ban is "hypocrisy at
its worst as it brings on the very 'evil' they say they abhor."
Farrel notes that women (and girls) who do not use birth
control end up pregnant and often choose to abort. Many
abortion supporters suspect that the religious organizations
have a hidden agenda: to impose their moral code on others
in regard to sexual conduct, and that pregnancy is the price
women pay for their moral turpitude.

Pro-choice advocates contend that the will of some religious individuals to impose their beliefs on others is seen in
the legislation of 49 states as they pass laws that slowly erode
abortion rights. *Roe v. Wade* prohibits states from banning
abortion, but many states seek to severely restrict access or
create obstacles for women. For instance, South Dakota now
has to fly doctors in from neighboring states to perform abortions because antiabortion protesters in this state have made it
impossible for doctors to set up their own clinics. Only 13
states prohibit most forms of protests at clinics, and many
states have imposed waiting periods and counseling requirements before women may have an abortion. In 2005, over 500
restrictive abortion laws were passed; in 2006, over 300 laws
were passed.

Pro-life supporters adamantly believe that life begins at
the moment of conception and that abortion is nothing short
of murder. They contend that just because the Court deems
abortion legal, this does not make it moral. Many of them do
not support abortion in any circumstance, including rape or
incest, or when the mother's life is in danger. Nellie Gray,
president of March for Life, asserts that the "state of a person
can never justify the intentional killing of an innocent born or
pre-born human in existence at fertilization. No exception! No
compromise!" Pro-life members can be seen at abortion clin-

ics protesting abortion and urging the patients to consider the alternatives, such as adoption or keeping the child. They have often been criticized for displaying grotesque pictures of aborted babies, but defend this tactic as a necessity to counteract claims that a fetus is just a blob of tissue.

Pro-life members work diligently to promote the perception that the unborn, regardless of its stage of development, is worthy of personhood. Their successful efforts are reflected in the surge of recent laws that afford the unborn the status of victim if they are injured or die as a result of another person's negligence or criminal intent. For example, in 2004, the California Supreme Court upheld the conviction of Howard Taylor for two counts of murder when he shot and killed a woman who was 11–13 weeks pregnant, even though he did not know that the woman was pregnant. On April 1, 2004, President George W. Bush signed the Unborn Victims of Violence Act, which recognizes unborn children as victims when they are injured or killed during the commission of federal or military crimes of violence. In remarks before signing the bill, the president said, "As these [present] and the other families understand, any time an expectant mother is a victim of violence, two lives are in the balance, each deserving protection, and each deserving justice. If the crime is murder and the unborn child's life ends, justice demands a full accounting under the law."

Religious organizations, too, are dispensing consequences to members who disregard the lives of the unborn. The Reverend Peter J. Jugis, bishop of Charlotte, North Carolina, no longer allows communion to church members who support abortion. He concludes that those individuals, along with lawmakers who support abortion, create serious harm to society by promoting evil in the United States, stating that procured abortion is "intrinsically evil and can never be justified." In addition to religious grounds, pro-life supporters also allege that women are led astray with lies and deception by the pro-choice groups. They contend that abortions are not safe, and point to statistics that indicate that one in 500 abortion patients will either die or be maimed. Additionally, fathers are not given a voice or choice if a woman decides to abort.

Regardless if abortion is legal, or will one day be illegal, the conflicting claims and assertions by both sides of this controversy may never be reconciled. Incompatible belief systems, values, and priorities ensure continued conflict. These incongruities form the foundation of *The Abortion Controversy* and the fallout that surrounds the issues of morality, rights, access to abortion, protests, and embryonic stem cell research.

CHAPTER 1

Is Abortion Immoral?

Deciding Abortion: An Overview

Daniel Oliver

Daniel Oliver is a senior director at the White House Writers Group in Washington, D.C. He was chairman of the Federal Trade Commission from 1986 to 1989.

The pro-abortion and anti abortion forces are warships passing in the night. Their slogans, "pro-choice" and "pro-life," don't engage the central issue that divides them, which is, what actually happens in an abortion. Neither group really disagrees with the other's slogan. None of the opponents of abortion would object to a woman's choosing to do what she wanted with a tumor or some other unwanted tissue growing on or in her body. On that issue they would be pro-choice. And no ordinary supporter of abortion would argue that a woman has a right to choose to do what she wants with her grandmother, or her infant daughter. In those cases, they would be pro life, not pro-choice.

Fetus versus Personhood

Nor was "choice"—understood as a woman's right to choose to terminate the life of a person—authorized by the Supreme Court in *Roe v. Wade*. What the Court decided in that case was that during the period before the fetus was viable (which the Court, writing in 1973, said usually occurred at 28 weeks but could occur earlier, even at 24 weeks) a woman could not be prohibited from exercising her "right to privacy," which included choosing to have an abortion. The Court did not hold that a woman had an unqualified right to destroy something that was a person. "If the State is interested in protecting fetal life after viability, it may go so far as to proscribe abortion during that period, except when it is necessary to preserve the life or health of the mother." The Court went on, in another decision handed down the same day, to define "health" so expansively as to put severe limits on states' practical ability to protect fetal life after viability. But that holding does not alter the fact that the Court has never explicitly held that a woman has an absolute right to destroy something that it recognizes as a person.

What was particularly provocative in the Court's decision was its "legislating" its own definition of life, i.e., "viability," despite a disingenuous disclaimer ("We need not resolve the difficult question of when life begins"). By not calling the fetus "life," the Court could pretend that it had not authorized the destruction of life.

Neither "life" nor "choice," therefore, is really the issue in the abortion dispute. And when we talk about "life" or "human life" we really mean "human being" or "person," as in Mother Teresa or Yasser Arafat—or "personhood," i.e., the nature of someone essentially like us and entitled to the same protection of the law.

The first and central issue in the abortion debate is whether the fetus is a person. The second issue is how we should behave if we can't conclusively decide the first issue. Is a fetus a person or simply part of the body of the woman in which it resides? What is life or personhood, and when does it begin? Is it something we ourselves define—as an umpire calls balls and strikes, which are neither balls nor strikes till he calls them? Or is life something that exists independent of whatever we mortals may think?

If life is only what we say it is, and begins only when we say it does, then—acting through the state—we can say anything we like and we can never be incorrect. We could say life begins when a child turns two. We could always change our minds, and legislate a different definition, but we could not then say that the previous definition had been incorrect. Of course, if the state cannot be incorrect in defining the fetus as not-a-life, it can also not be incorrect in defining a black person as not-a-life or not-a-person. We tried that once, but subsequently found that definition objectionable. Not just incorrect, but morally wrong.

We need to find a secular principle that will guide our behavior.

Alternatively, we can agree that the existence of life is independent of whatever we may think, and see our task as trying to determine, as opposed to defining, when life exists. Two places we could look to for guidance in making that determination are tradition and science. Civilized states have for generations considered the fetus a person. But that tradition is often regarded as suspect—a vestige of religious morality in the post-religious polity. Science also turns out not to be much help. The issue in dispute is not whether that-which-is-growing-inside-the-woman, at whatever stage it has reached (and for simplicity's sake I will call that entity a "fetus"), is some kind of life. Science agrees it is alive and that it has the DNA of the human species, and DNA distinct from its mother's. The science of statistics can tell us (and did tell the Supreme Court) when a fetus, on average, is viable outside the womb, and medical science can move, and since *Roe v. Wade* has moved, that date earlier. But viability becomes the factor that determines whether the fetus is a person only if we, the people, say it is—or if we, the people, let the Supreme Court say it is. Science itself does not tell us whether the fetus is a person.

A Secular Solution

If neither tradition nor science can tell us whether the fetus is a person, what should guide us in deciding whether to allow abortions? What should we do when we don't know something and have no way of figuring it out? We need to find a secular principle that will guide our behavior.

There are two possible errors that can be made in legislating that behavioral decision. One is allowing abortions if the fetus is a person. Why that is an error requires no explanation. The other is prohibiting abortions if the fetus is not a person. That would be an error because we, through the apparatus of the state, would have interfered for no valid reason with the right of a person to choose to act in accordance with her own wishes.

But the two possible errors are not equally culpable. Making a mistake that results in killing a human being is more culpable than making a mistake that only prohibits someone from removing a growth in her body, even if that prohibition results in emotional or financial distress. Even people who support abortion should agree with that.

Now let's try a thought experiment. Suppose a building is to be demolished as part of a program to construct free housing for the poor. Millions of dollars and many months have been spent preparing for the demolition of the building. Any additional delay, by even a single hour, will result in huge costs. The building has been carefully inspected to be sure that no one is in it. Demolition Day arrives, but moments before the explosive charges are to be detonated, a bystander cries out that he has spotted a figure moving at a window. A dozen others saw something too—but all agree that what they saw was a dog. Does demolition proceed? Probably, unless the animal-rights people can find an accommodating judge to block it. At the very least, the many millions spent and the benefits pending would be weighed against the life of the dog.

But now suppose a dozen different people, all credible citizens, say they were watching the same window and are certain that what they saw was not a dog, but a small boy. What would be done? Can there be any doubt? If there were any chance that the life seen in the building was human, demolition would not proceed. The millions spent would count for nothing. Everyone would apply an innate "precautionary principle" and not accept the risk of killing a human being.

We have to make a choice, while not knowing whether the fetus is a human being.

The Precautionary Principle

The Precautionary Principle is currently being used by many to counter the current presumption in favor of developing new technologies and products. The Precautionary Principle states that scientific certainty of harm is not required as a prerequisite for taking action to avert it. The most widely cited version of this principle in the environmental context is Principle 15 of the 1992 Rio Declaration on Environment and Development: "Where there are threats of serious or irreversible damage, lack of full scientific certainty shall not be used as a reason for postponing cost-effective measures to prevent environmental degradation."

That sentence applied to the abortion debate would read, "If there is a chance that a human being may be irreversibly damaged by an abortion, lack of certainty about the personhood of the fetus shall not be used as a reason for allowing abortions."

In the case of demolishing the building, in our thought experiment, the precautionary principle that resides in each of us would lead us all to opt for life: If in doubt, take no chance of killing a human being. Isn't that the situation with abortion? We have to make a choice, while not knowing whether the fetus is a human being. Those who do not oppose abortion should ask themselves how they can be sure the fetus is not a person, and why they are willing to risk being wrong on such an important matter. And those who oppose abortion should spend less time talking about being pro-life and more time asking how we should decide how to behave in the absence of certain knowledge about the humanity of the fetus.

Selective Abortion Is Immoral

Patricia E. Bauer

Patricia E. Bauer is a former Washington Post *reporter and bureau chief.*

If it's unacceptable for William Bennett to link abortion even conversationally with a whole class of people (and, of course, it is), why then do we as a society view abortion as justified and unremarkable in the case of another class of people: children with disabilities?

I have struggled with this question almost since our daughter Margaret was born, since she opened her big blue eyes and we got our first inkling that there was a full-fledged person behind them.

Whenever I am out with Margaret, I'm conscious that she represents a group whose ranks are shrinking because of the wide availability of prenatal testing and abortion. I don't know how many pregnancies are terminated because of prenatal diagnoses of Down syndrome, but some studies estimate 80 to 90 percent.

Imagine. As Margaret bounces through life, especially out here in the land of the perfect body, I see the way people look at her: curious, surprised, sometimes wary, occasionally disapproving or alarmed. I know that most women of childbearing age that we may encounter have judged her and her cohort, and have found their lives to be not worth living.

To them, Margaret falls into the category of avoidable human suffering. At best, a tragic mistake. At worst, a living embodiment of the pro-life movement. Less than human. A drain on society. That someone I love is regarded this way is unspeakably painful to me.

Selective Abortion Is Not a Moral Obligation

This view is probably particularly pronounced here in blue-state California, but I keep finding it everywhere, from academia on down. At a dinner party not long ago, I was seated next to the director of an Ivy League ethics program. In answer to another guest's question, he said he believes that prospective parents have a moral obligation to undergo prenatal testing and to terminate their pregnancy to avoid bringing forth a child with a disability, because it was immoral to subject a child to the kind of suffering he or she would have to endure. (When I started to pipe up about our family's experience, he smiled politely and turned to the lady on his left.)

In ancient Greece, babies with disabilities were left out in the elements to die.

Margaret does not view her life as unremitting human suffering (although she is angry that I haven't bought her an iPod). She's consumed with more important things, like the performance of the Boston Red Sox in the playoffs and the dance she's going to this weekend. Oh sure, she wishes she could learn faster and had better math skills. So do I. But it doesn't ruin our day, much less our lives. It's the negative social attitudes that cause us to suffer.

Many young women, upon meeting us, have asked whether I had "the test." I interpret the question as a get-home-free card. If I say no, they figure, that means I'm a victim of circumstance, and therefore not implicitly repudiating the decision they may make to abort if they think there are disabilities involved. If yes, then it means I'm a right-wing antiabortion nut whose choices aren't relevant to their lives.

Either way, they win.

In ancient Greece, babies with disabilities were left out in the elements to die. We in America rely on prenatal genetic testing to make our selections in private, but the effect on society is the same.

We love and admire her because of who she is . . . not in-spite of it.

Margaret's old pediatrician tells me that years ago he used to have a steady stream of patients with Down syndrome. Not anymore. Where did they go, I wonder. On the west side of L.A. [Los Angeles], they aren't being born anymore, he says.

All People Have Value

The irony is that we live in a time when medical advances are profoundly changing what it means to live with disabilities. Years ago, people with Down Syndrome often were housed in institutions. Many were in poor health, had limited self-care and social skills, couldn't read, and died young. It was thought that all their problems were unavoidable, caused by their genetic anomaly.

Now it seems clear that these people were limited at least as much by institutionalization, low expectations, lack of education and poor health care as by their DNA. Today people with Down Syndrome are living much longer and healthier lives than they did even 20 years ago. Buoyed by the educational reforms of the past quarter-century, they are increasingly finishing high school, living more independently and holding jobs.

That's the rational pitch; here's the emotional one. Margaret is a person and a member of our family. She has my husband's eyes, my hair and my mother-in-law's sense of humor. We love and admire her because of who she is—feisty and zesty and full of life—not inspite of it. She enriches our lives. If we might not have chosen to welcome her into our family, given the choice, then that is a statement more about our ignorance than about her inherent worth.

What I don't understand is how we as a society can tacitly write off a whole group of people as having no value. I'd like to think that it's time to put that particular piece of baggage on the table and talk about it, but I'm not optimistic. People want what they want: a perfect baby, a perfect life. To which I say: Good luck. Or maybe, dream on.

And here's one more piece of un-discussable baggage: This question is a small but nonetheless significant part of what's driving the abortion discussion in this country. I have to think that there are many pro-choicers who, while paying obeisance to the rights of people with disabilities, want at the same time to preserve their right to ensure that no one with disabilities will be born into their own families. The abortion debate is not just about a woman's right to choose whether to have a baby; it's also about a woman's right to choose which baby she wants to have.

It Is Immoral to Treat Fetuses as Property

Carl Estabrook

Carl Estabrook teaches at the University of Illinois. He ran for Congress in 2002 on the Green Party ticket.

There is no orthodoxy more firmly fixed on the American political landscape than that opposition to abortion belongs on the Right, while "defense of abortion rights" is the linchpin of the Left. But a consideration of what Left and Right mean suggests that the conjunction may be accidental and only temporary. . . .

But if we want a consistent usage for the Left/Right distinction, we might think of political parties ranged along a line according to how authoritarian or democratic they are. The further Right one goes, the more authoritarian the parties, and the further Left, the more democratic. . . .

The commitment to democracy and an ever-widening franchise means that it has been the Left under this definition that has called attention to marginalized groups in the modern West. The historic task of the Left has been to include in political and civil society groups formerly excluded on the grounds that their full humanity was denied, e.g., Africans, Amerindians, and women.

Society Routinely Marginalizes the Unwanted

Most arguments that hold abortion to be an ethically-acceptable choice depend on the assertion that a fetus is not a fully human person, and, therefore, the rules about killing human beings (e.g., that killing can be justified in cases of self-

Carl Estabrook, "Roe v Wade: Thirty Years Later: Abortion and the Left," www.counter punch.org, January 17, 2003. Reproduced by permission.

defense) simply don't apply to the argument. (It's true that some recent defenses of abortion have begun from the premise that abortion means killing a human being: as the defender of civil liberties [American writer] Nat Hentoff puts it, it's finally hard to deny that "it's a baby.") Physical dependency—the fact that the fetus depends on its mother's body—is often, curiously enough, alleged as an indication of the less-than-full humanity of the unborn.

If the Left continues to draw out the implication of its principles, it will discover the marginalization of the unborn and unwanted as, for example, it discovered the marginalization of women in the first and second waves of feminism in the 19th and 20th centuries. And it's reasonable to suspect that the discovery will take as long and involve as many contradictions as that concerning women did—and does.

Much of the thinking that leads to the position that abortion is generally acceptable depends upon a capitalist view of ownership.

There are, of course, groups on the political Left who have drawn this conclusion. [American woman suffrage leader] Elizabeth Cady Stanton wrote to [American writer and reformer] Julia Ward Howe in 1873, "When we consider that women are treated as property, it is degrading to women that we should treat our children as property to be disposed of as we see fit." [American anarchist] Emma Goldman thought that abortion was an index of the general immiseration of the working class, and the [American] suffragist Alice Paul spoke of it as "the ultimate exploitation of women."

Contemporary groups with similar positions include the Seamless Garment Network, which organizes against war, the death penalty, and violence against women, within which they include abortion. A Feminists for Life group was expelled from NOW [National Organization for Women] for deviance on this issue, and there are a number of religious-based radical groups that are anti-abortion, such as that associated with the late [American activist] Philip Berrigan, the anti-nuclear direct-action group, Plowshares.

Ownership Status of a Fetus

But it's not just that the Left should oppose abortion if it is understood as it has wished to be for more than two centuries, as proposing the increasing democratization of human life. It should also do so because much of the thinking that leads to the position that abortion is generally acceptable depends upon a capitalist view of ownership, against which the Left is properly critical.

That the Left is opposed to capitalism should go without saying, although it's a bit abstractly theoretical. The Left stands for real democracy, and capitalism is fundamentally contradictory to democracy. . . .

But theory is always the last to know. Even though capitalism doesn't exist, our general view of society is no other than the ghost of deceased capitalism, sitting crowned upon the grave thereof. (It's happened before: arguments drawn from pre-capitalist societies, notably feudalism, still underlie much of the common law.) And ownership is surrounded with mystification in our understanding, because the modern ruling class is made up of those who claim to have this peculiar relationship to the means of production—they "own" them—rather than consisting of warriors, as in the feudal society, or drivers of slaves, as in the ancient world. And those who don't control productive property in our society are even spoken of by a massively misleading analogy as "owning" their own labor (which they must sell).

The Economics of Abortion

Abortion is, among other things, a matter of political economy. Practically all of my friends who've had abortions or seriously considered doing so—mostly privileged people—

have said that they acted for economic reasons, inability to afford the care of a child in the midst of a career being the principal one. It's our being caught in the cash nexus that dictates to the poor and well-to-do alike that abortion is necessary.

Even the approval of abortion by [President Richard] Nixon's Supreme Court—not generally men of the Left—depended in part on a calculus that abortion was cheaper than the adequate social services for which there was a popular demand a generation ago (*Roe v. Wade*, January 22, 1973). The justices were undoubtedly motivated by visions of an insistent "underclass," at home and abroad, in those days of fear of both revolutionary and demographic explosion. Like the US government officials contemporaneously pressing anti-natal polices on the Third World, they agreed with the remark (probably apocryphal) attributed to [Argentine revolutionary leader] Che Guevara, that "It's easier to kill a guerrilla in the womb than in the hills."

Some recent defenses of the moral legitimacy of abortion have shifted from arguments based on the non-humanity of unborn children (i.e., that the fetus is not human enough to have rights) to what in the US are called libertarian arguments—e.g., "I have the right to do what I want with my body (including the contents of my womb)." Defense of abortion on the basis of the ownership of one's own body is then similar to the right-wing account of "takings," which resists governmental attempts to limit what can be done with real estate.

Abortion Jeopardizes Fundamental Principles

But I don't *own* my body; I *am* my body. Talking of owning one's body arises from a malign mix of factitious capitalist theory and debased Christianity: I am then regarded as an immaterial mind/soul related to my body as the bus driver is to the bus—a ghost in a machine, in the classic phrase. (Some Christians seem to forget that the fundamental Christian doctrine is the resurrection of the body, not the immortality of the soul.) It's finally this distancing, dualist, indeed Manichean idea of the self that casts abortion into the capitalist discussion of ownership.

Defense of the general acceptability of abortion on the basis of one's ownership of one's body is a capitalist position that the Left should be skeptical of, on its fundamental principles. But it's certainly correct—if a little oddly put—to say that every person has rights over her or his body: inalienable rights indeed (which means you can't even give them away), to life, liberty, and the pursuit of happiness. The abortion argument reduces to the question of how many persons are involved.

Abortion Cannot Be Regarded as Immoral

Richard C. Carrier

Richard C. Carrier is a historian, philosopher, and writer. He has also taught classes and frequently speaks and debates before audiences around the country.

This opening argument against the immorality and illegality of abortion is simple, short and largely unoriginal: the arguments have all been voiced and heard a thousand times before. As will become apparent, the present argument leaves numerous fundamental assumptions as undefended givens. This is deliberate. The novelty of the present debate is that the positive position shall be taken by a secularist, whom I presume shares many assumptions in common with me, in particular some physicalist account of mind and existence, and a nontheological understanding of morality and law. Whether she will challenge any of these or other assumptions, which ones she will challenge, and how she will challenge them are the very mysteries that prompted me to enter this debate. As a result, important pieces of my argument, and sources of evidence, will inevitably appear in rebuttals. What I present now is essentially the reason that I, personally and at the present time, do not regard abortion as immoral and would not approve of outlawing it. . . .

Abortion Is Not Immoral

Given the facts as we can at present prove them to be, there is no good reason to regard abortion as immoral. To demonstrate this we must first explain what it means for something to be moral or immoral, and also what abortion is.

The foundation of every moral system is the combination of values with facts. To disagree on a point of morality can thus be a dispute about the facts (such as the circumstances and consequences of an action), or a dispute about values, or both. If a disagreement hinges on facts, one case or the other is vindicated when both sides honestly investigate and acknowledge the facts that can be known. If a disagreement hinges on values, inquiry must be made as to why each holds the values they do. Values are either the conclusions derived from certain facts in combination with certain other values, or else they are fundamental. Disputes over values that are the conclusions derived from certain facts in combination with certain other values are resolved as for all other moral disagreements—by investigating the facts more carefully.

Disputes over fundamental values, however, are irreconcilable. Both sides must agree to disagree, or develop a mutually agreeable compromise. It is even possible, within certain limits, to respect the individual moral sentiments of others even when we do not adopt those principles ourselves. But disputes that appear irreconcilable are not necessarily about fundamental values. They may simply result from either side failing to understand the reasons for either position, or from the inability to establish certain facts as true or false. Such cases must be resolved by first tolerating each other or working out a compromise, while continuing to logically analyze the dispute and to investigate the facts. . . .

It is thus possible for abortion to be "immoral" for some but not all people

---

Those who argue that abortion is wrong generally base their argument on respect for individual human existence. Usually, this value, or something similar, is rightly assumed to be universally shared, and then the dispute arises only on matters of fact. I will continue this assumption. There are those, we can imagine, who not only have no value for respecting individual human existence, but also could not even in principle be persuaded to adopt such a value (e.g., by appealing to some other values they did possess which would be fulfilled by adopting a value for human life). But such people would not be persuadable on any point of morality anyway, rendering this debate of no use or interest to such a creature. We are thus speaking to, and for, everyone else. . . .

Digression on Moral Relativism

Something must first be said briefly about the moral subjectivism inherent in this analysis. . . . Some things could be "immoral" for some people and "moral" (or amoral) for others, since people vary in their values. For example, some people may possess a fundamental value for all animal life of any kind, which would entail not eating meat, not allowing suicide, nor even allowing the removal of life support for a brain-dead patient. But this value system would only exist for them, not for others. However, my analysis does not entail moral relativism in the usual sense, since it is also possible (and I believe it is the case) that some fundamental values are shared by all people, or very nearly all people (I allow some rare exceptions for the sociopath, who is generally regarded as having a mind alien to the vast majority of humankind, devoid of all ordinary moral sentiment).

If the above is true, it follows that there is a universal moral truth for everyone (or every sane person), a truth which derives from this set of shared values, whatever it happens to be. And this universal moral truth would exist side by side with other quasi-moral principles derived from non-universal values, shared within various groups or not shared at all. It is thus possible for abortion to be "immoral" for some but not all people, in this sense—just as it is possible for eating pork to be "immoral" for some but not all people. However, it might be better to call such things principles rather than morals, in order to reserve the title "morals" for only those principles that are universal (or would be universal, if everyone knew all the facts and all the ways these facts interacted with their values). From now on, when I employ the term "moral" or its cognates, I am referring to this universal truth, and not to the equally true but necessarily parochial principles found everywhere in human society. . . .

To put this all simply, the proposition "abortion is immoral" means to me that every non-sociopathic human being has some value which is contradicted or undermined by the practice of abortion, even if they are unaware of this contradiction. My position is thus that such a value does not exist, with respect to abortion, as the facts are presently understood. . . .

An abortion at this stage [embryo] is clearly a very different affair than at later stages.

Most abortions are conducted before the 85th day (within the first trimester). An abortion conducted between the 85th and 134th day of a pregnancy (second trimester) is formally called a "late-term abortion." Recent invention in political circles of the term "partial-birth abortion" refers not to abortion at all, but to the killing of a premature (third trimester) baby who is considered to have a remote chance of survival outside the womb. Such a procedure is almost unheard of and is conducted only under the most unusual of circumstances, such as when a baby is already dead, or cannot be prematurely delivered—due to deformity or injury of the womb or birth canal—but must still be removed to save the mother's life. . . .

The Essential Nature of Abortion

The immediate and obvious effect of abortion is the killing of a developing human organism. What this actually entails varies according to stage of development. As of fertilization there exists a zygote (a single cell with the genetic blueprint for constructing a unique person) which begins travelling towards the uterus, taking roughly three days to reach it. In this period, the zygote grows into a mass of sixty or more identical (undifferentiated) cells. Another two or three days and this mass begins to form an embryo (meaning that some simple differentiation occurs among the cells) and attaches to the uterine wall. It is this event which birth control medications prevent, if they first fail to prevent ovulation or fertilization. An abortion at this stage is clearly a very different affair than at later stages.

Given that abortion ... does not violate anyone's rights ... there is no good reason to make abortion illegal

---

Nerve cells do not appear until the third week, and though full cellular differentiation occurs in the fourth week, no functioning organs appear until the end of the second month, at which point the entire embryo is little more than an inch long, and is now formally called a "fetus" because preliminary organ development is complete and most of the remaining development is a matter of mere growth in size. At that stage, simple reflex nerve-muscle action is possible (the sort of event that doctors test for in adults by striking the knee with a hammer), and electricity can be conducted just as it can in a disembodied nerve cell. But the fetus does not become truly neurologically active until the fifth month (an event we call "quickening"). This activity might only be a generative one, i.e., the spontaneous nerve pulses could merely be autonomous or spontaneous reflexes aimed at stimulating and developing muscle and organ tissue. Nevertheless, it is in this month that a complex cerebral cortex, the one unique feature of human—in contrast with animal—brains, begins to develop, and is typically complete, though still growing, by the sixth month.

What is actually going on mentally at that point is unknown, but the hardware is in place for a human mind to exist in at least a primitive state.

The great majority of elective abortions occur before the fourth month begins, and there is effectively no such thing as an elective abortion in the fifth month or later. No competent doctor would advise it, no intelligent mother would risk it. . . .

Individual Human Existence

Until the 20th week, the cut-off date for an actual "abortion" to occur, there is no complex cerebral cortex and no major central nervous activity. That is a condition universally regarded as a state of death in adults. An *adult* human being in such a state cannot really be "killed," just unplugged. And such an act would not be disrespectful of their individual existence because that existence has already ceased, and only a body remains. Even if we were able to regenerate a brain-dead patient's cerebral cortex, using the genetic blueprint in her cells, we would still fail to resurrect her. We would instead merely create an identical twin inside a used body, with an infantile mind and no memories, no complex personality traits, and no intellectual skills. Although this fresh brain would be ready to learn and develop anew, it would be a different person. None of the unique features of the deceased would exist any more—the only mental features that would survive are the very same features that would be shared by any natural identical twins.

The fetus, before quickening, is in the very same state as this hypothetical regenerated person. And the analogy of identical twins is a crucial one. Twins share the exact same blueprint for brain and body, and there is nothing "individual" about a blueprint that can be shared by more than one individual person—their individuality does not derive from their blueprint, but from their unique personal development, which begins almost certainly before birth, but without any doubt upon birth, when there can be no mistake that novel sensory data has begun transforming the brain and educating it in unique ways. None of this individualization can occur before the existence of a complex cortex that can be individualized (pre-fifth-month)—certainly none before there is a central nerve organ of any kind (pre-third-month). Therefore, an individual human (as opposed to a vacant body) cannot exist when a medically-defined abortion occurs. This entails that abortion cannot counter our shared value for individual human existence. . . .

Given that abortion—an elective termination of pregnancy before the 20th week—does not violate anyone's rights and does no substantial harm, and actually performs some limited positive good, there is no good reason to make abortion illegal.

Abortion Does No Harm

From a point of view outside of this affair, the killing of a neurologically inactive fetus is no greater a harm than the killing of a mouse, and in fact decidedly less—a mouse is neurologically active, and though it lacks a complex cerebral cortex, it has a brain of suitable complexity to perceive pain (and I would argue that the mouse deserves some moral consideration, though less than humans). A fetus cannot perceive pain (and perception is not quite the same thing as sensation: sensation can exist without a brain, but perception cannot). The neural structures necessary to register and record sensations of pain transmitted by the appropriate nerves either do not exist or are not functioning before the fifth month of gestation. A fetus can no more feel pain than a surgical patient under general anesthesia, or a paraplegic whose lower-body nerves continue reacting to stimuli, but cease sending signals to the brain. And we have already established that a fetus does not contain an individual human personality of any kind, any more than a brain-dead adult does. With no perception of pain, and no loss of an individual personality, the act of abortion causes no immediate harm.

However, there may be indirect harm caused by abortion. For instance, there may be unacceptable medical risks to the mother, as there always are with any surgical procedure, even surgery of the outpatient variety. But I doubt such risks are unacceptable enough to warrant making the procedure illegal. . . .

An act that causes no involuntary harm and produces some benefits for individuals and society in general should never be outlawed.

Abortion Performs a Limited Positive Good

First, abortion is a notable benefit to society. The harm to a society that is caused by an excess of unchecked population growth is severe and well-documented. The ability of societies to check population growth without legalizing abortion has proven nearly non-existent: there are few countries in which abortion is outlawed or stigmatized that are not suffering harshly from overcrowding, with all the attendant economic, criminal, or political troubles. In contrast, most nations that allow the procedure are maintaining stable populations with nearly zero growth, and exhibiting more or less general prosperity. From a purely pragmatic perspective aimed at the interests of the commonwealth, abortion is at best a great benefit to mankind and at worst a necessary evil. And for women who regard zero growth as a moral imperative, abortion can even be a moral necessity from their point of view—although this would be better called a matter of principle, so as to distinguish this personal belief from the morally universal.

Second, abortion is a significant benefit for the individual woman. The risks of death or permanent disability certainly must be greater for a woman who carries a fetus to term and bears a child, prematurely or not, than for a woman who aborts before the third trimester of her pregnancy. And the social and economic ruin that can ensue from an untimely motherhood is a serious harm as well, and although this could be alleviated by recourse to adoption, free medical care for pregnant women, and public welfare for women unable to work as a consequence of their pregnancy, these solutions are not as simple as they sound, and are not so universally available as people might think. . . . Moreover, the potential physical harm from bearing a child simply cannot be alleviated. Abortion thus supplies some benefit for many women.

The Appropriate Legal Status of Abortion

An act that causes no involuntary harm and produces some benefits for individuals and society in general should never be outlawed. This is based on the principle that laws should only exist to preserve and protect the liberty of individuals and, when no liberty is at stake either way, to increase the general welfare of all citizens. Whether that principle is misinformed remains to be seen. But from the above analysis, there appears no way in which outlawing abortion would even indirectly preserve or protect the liberty of any individual, or provide any general benefit to the citizen body without uneccessarily depriving individuals of their liberty.

Religion Does Not Condemn Abortion

Freedom from Religion Foundation

The Freedom from Religion Foundation, Inc., incorporated in 1978, is a nonprofit educational group. Its purposes are to promote the constitutional principle of separation of state and church, and to educate the public on matters relating to nontheism.

What does the Bible say about abortion? Absolutely nothing! The word "abortion" does not appear in any translation of the bible!

Out of more than 600 laws of Moses, none comments on abortion. One Mosaic law about miscarriage specifically contradicts the claim that the bible is antiabortion, clearly stating that miscarriage does not involve the death of a human being. If a woman has a miscarriage as the result of a fight, the man who caused it should be fined. If the woman dies, however, the culprit must be killed:

"If men strive, and hurt a woman with child, so that her fruit depart from her, and yet no mischief follow: he shall be surely punished according as the woman's husband will lay upon him; and he shall pay as the judges determine.

"And if any mischief follow, then thou shalt give life for life, Eye for eye, tooth for tooth. . . ."—*Exod. 21:22–25*

The bible orders the death penalty for murder of a human being, but not for the expulsion of a fetus.

According to the bible, life begins at birth—when a baby draws its first breath. The bible defines life as "breath" in several significant passages, including the story of Adam's creation in Genesis 2:7, when God "breathed into his nostrils the breath of life; and man became a living soul." Jewish law traditionally considers that personhood begins at birth.

Desperate for a biblical basis for their beliefs, some antiabortionists cite obscure passages, usually metaphors or poetic phrasing, such as: "Behold, I was shapen in iniquity; and in sin did my mother conceive me" (Psalms 51:5). This is sexist, but does nothing other than to invoke original sin. It says nothing about abortion.

The Commandments, Moses, Jesus and Paul ignored every chance to condemn abortion. If abortion was an important concern, why didn't the bible say so?

Thou Shalt Not Kill

Many antiabortionists quote the sixth commandment, "Thou shalt not kill" (Exod. 20:13), as evidence that the bible is antiabortion. They fail to investigate the bible's definition of life (breath) or its deafening silence on abortion. Moreover, the Mosaic law in Exodus 21:22–25, directly following the Ten Commandments, makes it clear that an embryo or fetus is not a human being.

Far from demonstrating a "pro-life" attitude, the bible decimates innocent babies and pregnant women in passage after gory passage.

An honest reader must admit that the bible contradicts itself. "Thou shalt not kill" did not apply to many living, breathing human beings, including children, who are routinely massacred in the bible. The Mosaic law orders "Thou shalt kill" people for committing such "crimes" as cursing one's father or mother (Exod. 21:17), for being a "stubborn son" (Deut. 21:18–21), for being a homosexual (Lev. 20:13), or even for picking up sticks on the Sabbath (Numbers 15:32–35)! Far from protecting the sanctity of life, the bible promotes capital punishment for conduct which no civilized person or nation would regard as criminal.

Mass killings were routinely ordered, committed or approved by the God of the bible. One typical example is Numbers 25:4–9, when the Lord casually orders Moses to massacre 24,000 Israelites: "Take all the heads of the people, and hang them up before the Lord against the sun." Clearly, the bible is not pro-life!

Most scholars and translators agree that the injunction against killing forbade only the murder of (already born) Hebrews. It was open season on everyone else, including children, pregnant women and newborn babies.

The Bible Targets Children

"Happy shall he be, that taketh and dasheth thy little ones against the stones."—*Psalms 137:9* The bible is not pro-child. Why did God set a bear upon 42 children just for teasing a prophet (2 Kings 2:23–24)? Far from demonstrating a "pro-life" attitude, the bible decimates innocent babies and pregnant women in passage after gory passage, starting with the flood and the wanton destruction of Sodom and Gomorrah, progressing to the murder of the firstborn child of every household in Egypt (Exod. 12:29), and the New Testament threats of annihilation.

Space permits only a small sampling of biblical commandments or threats to kill children:

- **Numbers 31:17** Now therefore kill every male among the little ones.

- **Deuteronomy 2:34** Utterly destroyed the men and the women and the little ones.

- **Deuteronomy 28:53** And thou shalt eat the fruit of thine own body, the flesh of thy sons and of thy daughters.

- **1 Samuel 15:3** Slay both man and woman, infant and suckling.

- **2 Kings 8:12** Dash their children, and rip up their women with child.

- **2 Kings 15:16** All the women therein that were with child he ripped up.

- **Isaiah 13:16** Their children also shall be dashed to pieces before their eyes; their houses shall be spoiled and their wives ravished.

- **Isaiah 13:18** They shall have no pity on the fruit of the womb; their eyes shall not spare children.

- **Lamentations 2:20** Shall the women eat their fruit, and children.

- **Ezekiel 9:6** Slay utterly old and young, both maids and little children.

- **Hosea 9:14** Give them a miscarrying womb and dry breasts.

- **Hosea 13:16** Their infants shall be dashed in pieces, and their women with child shall be ripped up.

Then there are the dire warnings of Jesus in the New Testament:

> For, behold, the days are coming, in which they shall say, Blessed are the barren, and the womb that never bare, and the paps which never gave suck.—*Luke 23:29*

The teachings and contradictions of the bible show that antiabortionists do not have a "scriptural base" for their claim that their deity is "pro-life." Spontaneous abortions occur far more often than medical abortions. Gynecology textbooks conservatively cite a 15% miscarriage rate, with one medical study finding a spontaneous abortion rate of almost 90% in very early pregnancy. That would make a deity in charge of nature the greatest abortionist in history!

The Hidden Agenda

The bible is neither antiabortion nor pro-life, but does provide a biblical basis for the real motivation behind the antiabortion religious crusade: hatred of women. The bible is anti-woman, blaming women for sin, demanding subservience, mandating a slave/master relationship to men, and demonstrating contempt and lack of compassion:

> I will greatly multiply thy sorrow and thy conception; in sorrow thou shalt bring forth children; and thy desire shall be to thy husband, and he shall rule over thee.—*Genesis 3:16*

What self-respecting woman today would submit willingly to such tyranny?

The antiabortion position does not demonstrate love for humanity, or compassion for real human beings. Worldwatch Institute statistics show that 50% of abortions worldwide are illegal, and that at least 200,000 women die every year—and thousands more are hurt and maimed—from illegal or self-induced abortions. Unwanted pregnancies and complications from multiple pregnancies are a leading killer of women. Why do antiabortionists want North American women to join these ghastly mortality statistics? Every day around the world more than 40,000 people, mostly children, die from starvation or malnutrition. We must protect and cherish the right to life of the already-born.

Churches Support Abortion Rights

Numerous Christian denominations and religious groups agree that the bible does not condemn abortion and that abortion should continue to be legal. These include:

- American Baptist Churches–USA

- American Ethical Union

- American Friends (Quaker) Service Committee

- American Jewish Congress

- Christian Church (Disciples of Christ)

- Episcopal Church

- Lutheran Women's Caucus

- Moravian Church in America–Northern Province

- Presbyterian Church (USA)

- Reorganized Church of Jesus Christ of Latter Day Saints

- Union of American Hebrew Congregations

- Unitarian Universalist Association

- United Church of Christ

- United Methodist Church

- United Synagogue of America

- Women's Caucus Church of the Brethren

- YWCA

- Religious Coalition for Reproductive Choice

- Catholics for Free Choice

- Evangelicals for Choice

Belief that "a human being exists at conception" is a matter of faith, not fact. Legislating antiabortion faith would be as immoral and un-American as passing a law that all citizens must attend Catholic mass!

The bible does not condemn abortion; but even if it did, we live under a secular constitution, not in a theocracy. The separation of church and state, the right to privacy, and women's rights all demand freedom of choice.

CHAPTER 2

Should Abortion Rights Be Protected or Restricted?

Chapter Preface

Kimberly was home alone with her two sleeping children when her estranged husband came to the house, high on drugs, and began arguing about child support payments. Before he left, he raped her. Two weeks later, Kimberly discovered she was pregnant. She was out of work and broke. She feared that her husband would kill her if she kept the baby. Her pregnancy progressed as she desperately tried to save enough money to pay for an abortion. The further along her pregnancy, the more expensive the abortion was. At the same time, various states and Congress were working to pass laws that would restrict access to abortion.

Kimberly is typical of many women who seek an abortion: Approximately 60 percent are mothers, 57 percent are poor, and 78 percent are religious. Yet, if abortion is not legal or is difficult to obtain, many of these women will resort to so-called back alley abortions, possibly risking their lives or facing severe injury. It is estimated that 700,000 women underwent illegal abortions in the United States in the 1950s and 1960s.

Many individuals and organizations are now fighting hard to restrict or eliminate all legal abortions. As they do so, remnants of backstreet abortions are starting to reemerge. There are now Web sites that give detailed instruction on how to perform an abortion. In El Salvador, where abortion patients and their doctors face up to 50 years in prison, word-of-mouth and Web sites detail how to use an ulcer medicine to produce an abortion.

Abortion supporters assert that women who seek abortions are not cruel monsters; they are desperate women in desperate circumstances. There are also women who do not want to bring babies into this world who would suffer from debilitating defects, such as spina bifida or severe mental retardation. For these women, abortion is an act of mercy. Not so, says pro-lifers. They believe that all life is worthy and maintain that people should not be playing God by determining who is or is not fit to live.

In addition to adult women finding it difficult to locate an abortion provider, teen girls are encountering even more difficulties. Many states are now passing laws that prohibit teens from getting an abortion without parental consent; some states allow for a judicial review if the girl does not want to tell her parents. Abortion supporters believe these laws put the girls in jeopardy of abuse from their parents; in some cases pregnancy is a result of molestation by a family member. Supporters of parental consent laws maintain that these laws are needed to protect the health of the girls; parents are more likely to monitor the girls' health after an abortion, thereby reducing the chance of life-threatening complications.

Pro-life proponents contend that abortion is immoral, degrading to women, and a social failure that undermines the good of society. They dispute the number of illegal abortions and maintain that most women would not seek an abortion if it were illegal; instead, they would seek alternatives such as adoption or keeping the child. They point to studies that show that most Americans want to at least restrict abortions. Other studies show that abortion rates are down, but this may be attributed to better birth control methods and education, and also because fewer doctors and clinics are available today than there were in 1982. Additionally, almost half the states prohibit insurance coverage for abortions or mandate that women pay higher premiums for abortion coverage.

Former First Lady and now Senator Hillary Clinton stated that "the best way to reduce the number of abortions is to reduce the number of unwanted pregnancies in the first place." In order to do so, better birth control methods and availability of family planning services are needed. These options, however, are sometimes also opposed by those who oppose abortion. Against this backdrop, the authors in the following chapter argue the merits of protecting or restricting abortion rights.

Religious Groups Aim to Eliminate Women's Rights

Austin Cline

Austin Cline is actively involved in educating people about atheism and secular humanism on the Internet.

The most important issue for the Christian Right is criminalizing abortion. There is disagreement on the penalties for abortion (few want to treat it as murder, despite the rhetoric) and whether there should be exemptions (like for rape, incest, or the health of the mother), but there is agreement that abortion must end. There is no prospect of a total ban any time soon, so in the meantime they work on undermining it and hindering women's ability to actually obtain an abortion.

Women Are Treated Like Children

One means for undermining a woman's right to obtain an abortion is to deny her the ability to make the decision on her own. Minors are required to obtain permission from their parents or, in their absence, a judge. Adult women are required to at least notify their spouses—which, in some cases, is effectively the same as having to obtain permission. Women are thus informed that they can't be trusted to make these decisions without adults or men providing input and advice.

Another example of not trusting women to make decisions about abortion is the requirement that they go through counseling before undergoing the procedure. Required counseling assumes that women haven't given serious thought to all their options already. Sometimes, they are even plied with unscientific and false information, for example, about when

Austin Cline, "Undermining Abortion: How the Christian Right Undermines the Right to Abortion," atheism.about.com, March 15, 2006. Reproduced by permission.

the fetus might start experiencing pain. The entire purpose of these laws is to prevent women from choosing an abortion, not to educate and inform.

Distrust of women's ability to make decisions about having an abortion is also the basis for requiring waiting periods: women who come to an abortion clinic are forced to return days later to actually get an abortion. The ostensible reason is to give women time to reconsider their decision, as if they hadn't already thought deeply about it. The practical effect, surely recognized by those in charge, is that many women are unable to return and never get an abortion at all. That's the point.

If there are no clinics providing abortions, then women won't end up having abortions. Anti-choice activists know this very well and have invested tremendous resources into protesting at clinics. Women are too intimidated to go. Healthcare professionals are too intimidated to go to work. Doctors are too intimidated to go into providing abortions—fewer and fewer even learn to do them. Some states only have one clinic left. Some clinics have no permanent doctors.

Many forms of basic healthcare are funded, at least in part, by the government. Funding for abortion is banned, however. Even if someone works for the government, they won't get help paying to abort a fetus with fatal birth defects. The lack of funding for abortions can easily put them out of the reach of poor women who are likely seeking abortions because they cannot afford to care for more children. Ultimately, the state pays more to help these families.

Religious Views Are Forced on Our Secular Society

The Christian Right has demonstrated growing interest in "protecting" fetuses from various sorts of abuse. They want laws that treat attacks on women that lead to the death of the fetus as murder cases. They want to punish women who drink, smoke, or do drugs while pregnant. The point of all this is to establish in the law that a fetus is a person with rights—especially a right to live. If it's murder to attack a woman and kill her fetus, why not when a doctor kills the fetus in an abortion?

The consistent theme of all Christian Right policies on abortion is to undermine or eliminate the ability of women to exercise their right to obtain an abortion.

Short of criminalizing abortion completely, an important goal for the Christian Right is to have severe restrictions on when abortions can be performed and the reasons for which legal abortions are allowed. Initial steps would be to limit abortions to just the first trimester and to exclude women who want an abortion for "frivolous" reasons. Slow, small steps would lead us up to these changes and, over time, per-haps to eliminate abortion entirely.

The right to abortion and the right to contraception are more tightly connected than most people realize. Both are based on a right to privacy and control over one's body, so at-tacks on one implicate the other. The Christian Right focuses on abortion, but they have been paying more attention to contraception. This is not a truly separate issue for them—it's all part of a larger assault on sexual liberty in modern society.

Abortion Rights Are Undermined

The consistent theme of all Christian Right policies on abor-tion is to undermine or eliminate the ability of women to ex-ercise their right to obtain an abortion. Anti-choice activists certainly won't deny this, since their long-term goal is to end legalized abortion completely. We should, however, contem-plate what this means for the right to have an abortion itself.

Imagine if voting booths were only open for one hour a day and located far away from population centers. This wouldn't violate anything in the Constitution, so technically people would still have the right to vote, but what good is a right that you cannot exercise? For a significant number of women around the country, abortion services are as inaccessible as those hypothetical voting booths. Over 80% of all counties in America have no abortion services, so women have to travel some distance just to consult with a doctor—a significant hardship for poor women in rural areas. Then, they may be told that they have to return after a "waiting period" which government officials decided was necessary.

If women are denied the opportunities and resources to have an abortion, to what extent are we justified in saying that they have a right to an abortion in the first place? To make the right to abortion a genuine right, the government would have to assume the duty of protecting it—and that would arguably include ensuring that women have the resources and opportunities to get an abortion if that is what they wish. Even many supporters of abortion rights may balk at the prospect of the government helping to finance abortions, but that calls into question whether they really support abortion rights in the first place.

If someone only supports the "right" to abortion for women who can afford it, can afford the travel, and can afford the waiting times, isn't that a bit like supporting the "right" of people to vote if they can afford the costs of time and money to travel to distantly-located voting booths?

Legal Threats Aim to Undermine Abortion Rights

Karen O'Connor

Karen O'Connor is a professor of government at American University and the director of its nonpartisan Women & Politics Institute.

Good afternoon, Chairman Chabot, Representative Nadler, Members of the Subcommittee, and distinguished guests. My name is Karen O'Connor, and I am a Professor of Government at American University and the founder and Director of its nonpartisan Women & Politics Institute....

I am honored to testify regarding the significant implications of *Roe v. Wade* [1973] and *Doe v. Bolton* [1973] for American women and families. Today I will address the legal significance of *Roe v. Wade* and *Doe v. Bolton*, their strong constitutional underpinnings, their profound consequences for women's health and lives, and the legal and public health necessity of preserving a woman's right to choose abortion.... Reproductive freedom is truly at a crossroads.

Abortion History and Consequences

Abortion regulations and restrictions are not rooted in ancient theory or common law; despite the fact that abortion was common throughout history, no government—be it local, state, or national—attempted to regulate the practice until well into the nineteenth century. As Justice [Harry] Blackmun noted in *Roe v. Wade*, "at common law, at the time of the adoption of our Constitution, and throughout the major portion of the 19th century . . . a woman enjoyed a substantially

Karen O'Connor, "Testimony of Professor Karen O'Connor to U.S. House of Representatives Committee on the Judiciary Hearing Before the Subcommittee on the Constitution: The Scope and Myths of *Roe v. Wade*," judiciary.house.gov, March 2, 2006. Reproduced by permission of the author.

broader right to terminate a pregnancy than she does in most States today." Indeed, in 1812, a Massachusetts Court found that an abortion performed before "quickening," defined as the time when a woman begins to feel movement in utero, usually between the 16th and 18th week of pregnancy, was not punishable at law.

The first abortion restrictions enacted in the United States were state statutory creations that marked a shift away from common law. In 1821, Connecticut became the first state to criminalize abortion *after quickening.* By 1840, eight states had enacted statutory abortion restrictions. Other states quickly followed suit; by 1910 every state except Kentucky had made abortion a felony.

Illegal abortions ... put women at high risk of incomplete abortions, infection, and death.

By the early 1970s, however, following the lead of the American College of Obstetricians and Gynecologists and the American Law Institute (ALI), fourteen states liberalized their abortion statutes to permit abortion in limited circumstances: when the woman's health was in danger, when the woman was the victim of rape or incest, or when there was a likelihood of a fetal abnormality. Still, only four states—Alaska, Hawaii, New York, and Washington—had decriminalized the provision of abortion for any reason during the early stages of pregnancy.

Illegal Abortions Thrived

The fact that abortion was illegal in all but a few states prior to *Roe* did not mean, however, that women were not obtaining the procedure. Indeed, an 1871 American Medical Association report found that 20% of all pregnancies were deliberately terminated. It is estimated that anywhere from 200,000 to 1.2 million illegal or self-induced abortions were performed in the 1950s and 1960s. The general unavailability of *legal* abortions meant that the vast majority of women who wanted to terminate a pregnancy were left with only one "option": obtaining illegal and dangerous abortion procedures, commonly referred to as "back-alley abortions."

Illegal abortions, sometimes performed by lay people who did not have the proper training, equipment, or methods of anesthesia or sanitation, were extremely dangerous and put women at high risk of incomplete abortions, infection, and death. Estimates regarding the number of death and infections resulting from illegal or self-induced abortion are, of course, difficult to make given that many women, or their families in cases of the woman's death, were reluctant to attribute the infection or death to illegal abortion. Some estimate, however, that 5,000 women a year died from illegal, unsafe abortions before *Roe v. Wade*. In 1965, illegal abortion accounted for a *reported* 17 percent of all deaths due to pregnancy and childbirth. These burdens fell disproportionately on women of color: from 1972 to 1974, the mortality rate due to illegal abortions for non-white women was twelve times that for white women. And, none of these numbers include the thousands of women who willingly endured dangerous, invasive hysterectomies or tubal ligations to make certain that they would not have to have abortions should they have additional pregnancies.

Reproductive Freedom and Privacy

In 1973, against a background of increasing litigation surrounding contraception and abortion—and the horrifying reality that American mothers, sisters, and daughters were being forced into the back alleys—the Supreme Court granted *certiorari* in the companion cases of *Roe v. Wade* and *Doe v. Bolton*. Jane Roe, who we know today as Norma McCorvey, challenged a Texas abortion law that prohibited abortions in all cases except to save a woman's life. . . . Doe's lawyers, acting on her behalf as well as several doctors, nurses, clergy, and social workers, alleged that the Georgia law was an unconstitutional undue restriction of personal and marital privacy.

The right to privacy was well-recognized . . . decades before the Roe *decision.*

In a landmark 7 to 2 decision, the Supreme Court held that the "right of privacy . . . is broad enough to encompass a woman's decision whether or not to terminate her pregnancy." The Court also recognized that the decision of whether to have a child is unique to every woman and her life circumstances, and therefore must be a personal, individual decision.

> The detriment that the State would impose upon the pregnant woman by denying this choice altogether is apparent. Specific and direct harm medically diagnosable even in early pregnancy may be involved. Maternity, or additional offspring, may force upon the woman a distressful life and future. Psychological harm may be imminent. Mental and physical health may be taxed by child care. There is also the distress, for all concerned, associated with the unwanted child, and there is the problem of bringing a child into a family already unable, psychologically and otherwise, to care for it. In other cases, as in this one, the additional difficulties and continuing stigma of unwed motherhood may be involved. All these are factors the woman and her responsible physician necessarily will consider in consultation.

. . . The right to privacy so central in *Roe* was not "announced" for the first time in the *Roe* decision. Rather, in the decades prior to *Roe*, the Court defined the right to privacy as a fundamental freedom subject to exacting strict scrutiny by the Court.

The right to privacy was well-recognized—both in the reproductive freedom context and outside the reproductive freedom context—decades before the *Roe* decision. As the *Roe*

Court itself stated, "In a line of decisions . . . going back perhaps as far as [1891], the Court has recognized that a right of personal privacy, or a guarantee of certain areas or zones of privacy, does exist under the Constitution." . . .

Abortion Rights Give Women Reproductive Responsibility

Roe's implications for women were profound and wide-reaching. The most immediate result was to rescue women from the back alleys, making access to safe, legal abortion possible for women who chose it. Just as importantly, *Roe* marked a new beginning in women's ability to control their own fertility and to choose whether or not to have children. *Roe* recognized that the woman deciding whether to continue a pregnancy, and only that woman, must make the personal choice that is in keeping with her own religious, philosophical, and moral beliefs. This freedom of choice led to increased freedom in other areas; as the Supreme Court noted in 1992, "the ability of women to participate equally in the economic and social life of the Nation has been facilitated by their ability to control their reproductive lives."

Roe protects a woman's bodily integrity, but, just as importantly, protects a woman's right to be responsible for the choices she makes and the options she chooses. A woman's ability to decide when and if she will have children will ultimately make her a better mother, if she chooses to become one, and helps ensure that children are brought into families that are willing and able to both financially and emotionally care for them. A woman's ability to control her own reproduction ensures that she can make the medical decisions central to her physical and emotional well-being. And this autonomy allows women to make the choices we perhaps now take for granted: whether and when to marry, whether and when to have children, and whether to pursue educational opportunities or a professional career.

Continual Legal Battles with Anti-Abortion Bills

Legal and political attacks on *Roe* began even before the ink was dry on the decision. Within six months after *Roe* was decided, 188 anti-abortion bills were introduced in 41 state legislatures. State restrictions—such as waiting periods, spousal and parental consent requirements, and informed consent requirements—slowly chipped away at *Roe*'s protections, limiting abortion availability for all women. These restrictions fell most heavily on low-income women, especially young women and women of color, who, despite the legality of abortion, often could not access such services. For example, 33 states and the District of Columbia currently restrict low-income women's access to abortion; several federal laws, such as the Hyde Amendment, bar access to abortion care for low-income women who rely on the federal government for their health care, with exceptions only to preserve the woman's life or if the pregnancy results from rape or incest. Likewise, 44 states restrict young women's access to abortion by mandating parental notice or consent.

Roe recognized the right of a woman to make certain fundamental decisions affecting her destiny.

Battles over abortion continue to be waged in the states today. In 2005 alone, 614 anti-choice measures were considered in state legislatures. Moreover, every state with a regular legislative session, except the District of Columbia, considered anti-choice legislation in 2005: 77 of these legislative measures involved mandatory counseling and mandatory delay requirements for women seeking abortion services; 33 legislative measures would permit individuals and/or corporations to refuse to provide abortion, family planning, and other medical services; 60 legislative measures placed restrictions on young women's access to reproductive health services (including abortion and family planning); and 61 legislative measures were targeted regulations of abortion providers. Overall, 58 of these anti-choice measures were enacted—a 100% increase from 2004.

Tellingly, however, despite countless legal challenges, and thousands of legislative attacks on *Roe*, the Supreme Court has continually reaffirmed the continued validity and constitutionality of the basic principles articulated in the decision, recognizing that a woman's right to control her own body . . . remains just as fundamental today. . . . In *Lawrence v. Texas* [2003], the Court [stated] "*Roe* recognized the right of a woman to make certain fundamental decisions affecting her destiny and confirmed once more that the protection of liberty under the Due Process Clause has a substantive dimension of fundamental significance in defining the rights of the person." . . .

Banning Abortion Without Regard for Women's Health

Despite over thirty years of Supreme Court precedent reaffirming *Roe*, the past year [2005] has seen unprecedented—and unconscionable—attacks on the fundamental right to choose. Many of these most recent measures have been proposed or enacted without any regard for protecting a woman's health, a principle that has underpinned the Supreme Court's abortion jurisprudence for more than three decades. Just last week [February 2006], the South Dakota Senate passed a law, which is awaiting the Governor's signature, that would ban abortions in that state *at any stage in pregnancy*. The ban, in flat violation of Supreme Court precedent, does not contain any exception whatsoever to protect a woman's health, nor does it contain an exception for pregnancies that result from rape or incest. Similarly, in 2003, this Congress passed an abortion ban without any exception for women's health; every court to examine that ban has ruled that it is unconstitutional for this very reason. Just last week [February 2006], the Supreme Court granted review in one of those cases, setting the stage for a potential reversal of the Court's 2000 ruling on this issue. Just last year [2005], this very House of Representatives passed the Child Interstate Abortion Notification Act, which restricts a young woman access to abortion and demands parental involvement *even when the young woman's health is in danger or she has been the victim of rape or incest.*

Thus, despite the fact that history demonstrates that the unavailability of legal, safe abortion does not prevent abortion, but only leads women to seek unsafe abortions, it is abundantly clear that *Roe*'s protections are in jeopardy. Given President [George W.] Bush's appointment of two Supreme Court Justices who appear likely to be hostile to *Roe* and a woman's right to control her body, we can no longer be assured that the Supreme Court will protect the fundamental right to choose.

Re-criminalizing abortion . . . will not end the practice of abortion; it will simply end the practice of safe abortion.

What then, would happen if *Roe* were overturned? It is probable that many states would revive and enact immediate abortion bans. Four states (Alabama, Delaware, Massachusetts, and Wisconsin) have so-called "trigger" laws on their books, so named because they are "triggered" by the reversal of *Roe*, and would outlaw abortion immediately if the decision were overturned. Another thirteen states have abortion bans on the books that have been blocked by courts as unconstitutional. If *Roe* was overturned, officials in such states could immediately file suit asking a court to set aside the prior order that prevented enforcement of the state law. Even if states did not outlaw abortion entirely, they would be given free rein to restrict or ban abortion in a variety of circumstances if *Roe* were reversed. One need only look at the number of state restrictions placed on abortions in 2005, and the legislation that is likely to be enacted in South Dakota, to know this possibility is all too real.

Ultimately, abortion would likely remain legal in a small number of states, but even in such states, women's access to abortion would likely be severely restricted. This would create a daunting, patchwork system of abortion statutes: a woman's right to obtain an abortion would be entirely dependent on the state in which she lived or her ability to travel to another state—assuming the states that keep abortion legal would permit non-residents to obtain abortions in that state. For those women who are able to navigate this hodgepodge, the need to travel and the increased demand for a dwindling number of abortion providers could lead to dangerous delays in the provision of abortion care.

Reproductive Choices Are a Fundamental Right

Even more frightening, however, would be the plight of women who live in states where abortion is illegal or providers unavailable. In essence, overruling *Roe* would force a return to the two-tier system of abortion access that was in place before 1973: women with the financial ability to travel to other states may still be able to exercise their rights, while low-income women (disproportionately women of color and young women) would not. For these women, we would see a return to the days of back-alley and self-induced abortions; a return to the day where women—our daughters, our sisters, our mothers, and our wives—sacrificed their health and lives because they felt they were left with no other option. Recriminalizing abortion, or so severely restricting it so as to make it practically unavailable, will not end the practice of abortion; it will simply end the practice of *safe* abortion.

And, because the constitutional protections enunciated in *Roe* underpin so many other fundamental rights that are critical to women's health and well-being, *Roe*'s demise could open the door to future encroachments of these rights. For example, access to birth control also depends on the privacy right articulated in *Griswold* and echoed in *Roe*. The availability of contraception is critical to reducing unintended pregnancies, reducing the number of abortions, and improving the health of women and their children. The ultimate safety of these rights depends in large measure on the security of *Roe*.

I am a mother, a daughter, and a sister. The right to make private decisions to have sex or remain celibate, to use birth control or not, to resort to a safe and legal abortion if needed or to carry a pregnancy to term, has given women power over their destinies that women who came before me did not enjoy. As the Supreme Court so aptly stated in *Planned Parenthood v. Casey* [1992], "An entire generation has come of age free to assume *Roe*'s concept of liberty in defining the capacity of women to act in society, and to make reproductive decisions; no erosion of principle going to liberty or personal autonomy has left *Roe*'s central holding a doctrinal remnant; *Roe* portends no developments at odds with other precedent for the analysis of personal liberty. . . ."

Roe was not only a decision that legalized a medical procedure and protected women's health; it was—and is—a decision that gave a woman the option to make the reproductive choices that were right for her health, her family, and her life. No right can be more important or more fundamental than a woman's right to control her bodily integrity free from governmental interference—the right safeguarded by a very fragile, very threatened *Roe*.

Most Americans Favor Restrictions on Abortions

U.S. Conference of Catholic Bishops

The U.S. Conference of Catholic Bishops is an assembly of the Catholic Church hierarchy who work together to carry on Catholic activities in the United States.

Let not your hearts be troubled by polls showing support for *Roe v. Wade* or a "pro-choice" majority of Americans. Results like these are produced by questions that are biased (implying, for example, that *Roe* legalized only first-trimester abortions), imprecise or confusing. Sometimes all three.

Many polls ask whether abortion should be legal under most or only a few "*circumstances*" or "legal in most *cases*" versus "illegal in most *cases*." Words like cases, circumstances, most, some, and few can mean very different things to different people in the context of abortion. Under today's "dictatorship of relativism" (as Pope Benedict calls it), many Americans are apt to tell pollsters they can imagine valid exceptions to any moral norm.

A question such as "Would you like to see the Supreme Court overturn its 1973 *Roe v. Wade* decision concerning abortion, or not?" assumes that the respondent knows what *Roe* really entails and what the impact of its being overturned would be. A whopping 66% answered "no, do not overturn" (CNN/*USA Today*/Gallup, January 2006). Either two-thirds of Americans really do support abortion on demand throughout pregnancy or (much more likely) many of them do not realize that is what *Roe* produced. And many may think that the impact of overturning *Roe* would be automatically to outlaw all abortions throughout the United States. Advocacy groups exploit such misunderstandings to portray a future in which women are suddenly sent off to die from "coat hanger" or "back alley" abortions.

Most Americans Oppose Abortion

Why can we assume that most of the 66% of respondents expressing support for *Roe* are ill-informed? Because polls with precisely-worded questions based on identified circumstances, which are far better measures of public opinion, show waning support for the policy of *Roe*. A CBS News poll in January 2006, for example, asked "What are your personal feelings about abortion?" and offered four specific choices:

- abortion should only be permitted to save the woman's life (17%)

- it should be permitted only in cases of rape, incest and to save the woman's life (33%)

- it should be permitted, but subject to greater restrictions than it is now (15%) and

- it should be permitted in all cases (27%).

Alert readers will notice a category missing. The poll did not even offer the choice of "should never be permitted," which has garnered as much as 17% in other polls. Nevertheless, 5% of respondents volunteered that answer.

So the composite result is that (at least) 55% of Americans would ban all abortion, or restrict its legality to cases where the mother's life is at risk or the pregnancy resulted from rape or incest—all of which together make up less than 1.5% of abortions. And 70% of Americans want abortion to be subject to greater restrictions than it is now, whereas 27% who would keep abortion as it is under *Roe*.

These pro-life results are encouraging. This poll—by not offering the choice "should never be permitted"—even undercounts pro-life sentiment. An April 2005 poll by the polling company, inc.™ offered these six choices:

- never legal (17%)

- legal only when mother's life is in danger (14%)

- mother's life at risk plus cases of rape and incest (31%)

- legal for any reason during first 3 months only (21%)

- legal through 6 months (4%) and

- legal any time, any reason (10%).

To summarize, 62% of respondents would restrict abortion to the 1.5% of "hard cases," and only 10% favor the abortion regime established by *Roe* and *Planned Parenthood v. Casey*. And that's how we know that the 66% of Americans who answered "don't overturn *Roe*" in the poll mentioned earlier do not know *Roe*.

To summarize, 62% of respondents would restrict abortion to the 1.5% of 'hard cases.'

Strong Support for Abortion Restrictions

The most recent, and extraordinary, poll was conducted March 10–14, 2006, by Zogby International. The survey is unusual for the number and specificity of its questions on abortion, and for its breadth—30,117 respondents in the 48 contiguous states. Due to its size, the margin of error (MOE) was only 0.6%, significantly less than the standard 3–4% MOE in surveys of 1,000 people.

One reason for the survey was to test the relative strengths of the pro-life and pro-choice positions vis-à-vis hypothetical candidates in the 2006 and 2008 elections. Zogby concluded that "Democrats will have trouble gaining a political advantage by using the emotionally charged issue of abortion," as almost every question elicited a majority or plurality pro-life response.

The survey results are useful markers pointing to where the pro-life community has succeeded, where it can expect to be successful in the near future, and where greater educational efforts are needed.

One recent success: The pro-life outcry against a litmus test for judicial nominees based on allegiance to *Roe v. Wade*—widely reported and seconded by many national commentators—resonated with public opinion. By a margin of better than two-to-one (59% to 28%), respondents oppose the use of a filibuster based on a nominee's position on abortion. Only 18% of respondents say that *only* pro-choice nominees should be confirmed to the U.S. Supreme Court; 71% disagree.

Requiring parental notification for a minor to have an abortion is favored almost 2-to-1.

An area where greater educational efforts are called for: half of Americans have forgotten a basic lesson from high school biology:

- only 50% think human life begins at conception

- 9% think life begins at 3 months

- 8% at 6 months and

- 19% at birth.

Responding to another question, 59% of respondents agree (29% disagree) that abortion ends a human life. It appears that 29% of Americans define the beginning of a human life according to some standard other than biological reality. In doing so, they fail to see the danger of defining life based on outward appearance, or on some social or philosophical criteria like self-awareness or the ability to feed oneself. Efforts to correct such fallacies and to communicate the basic facts of human development would not be wasted.

The Zogby survey also gauged support for various prolife laws. Support continues to be strong for the most common state restrictions on abortion.

Requiring parental notification for a minor to have an abortion is favored almost 2-to-1 (59% approved, 32% opposed). Where such laws apply to all minors under 18, support drops slightly (55% vs. 36%); support rises to a 3-to-1 margin where such laws apply to minors under 16 years of age—69% vs. 23%.

Respondents approve of informed consent laws by a margin of 55% to 37%, and support 24-hour waiting period laws by an almost identical margin—56% to 37%. . . .

Teens' Abortions Are Restricted

Health and safety regulations for abortion clinics, mandatory reporting, restricting Medicaid funding, prohibiting insurance coverage of abortion, and the recent South Dakota ban on all abortion except when the mother's life is endangered are among the ways states are attempting to restrict or regulate abortion. . . .

Concerning abortions on minors, 26 states currently require the *consent* of one or both parents; 18 require parental *notification* only. In either case, laws generally contain an expedited judicial bypass procedure allowing the minor girl to avoid parental involvement. Courts have struck down four parental consent laws and five parental notice laws.

The answer is that parental involvement laws do reduce teen abortion rates.

The abortion lobby is adept at arguing "in the alternative." Logic and consistency have never been its hallmarks. Sometimes they say: Parental involvement laws unduly burden young women, preventing them from getting needed reproductive health care (read: abortion). Then they turn around and say: Parental involvement laws are a waste of time because they do *not* reduce abortions among minors. A recent *New York Times* front-page headline took the latter view, declaring "Scant Drop in Abortion Rates if Parents Are Told" (March 6, 2006). Plausible-looking statistics were presented to support this thesis. So what is it—waste of time, or an effective tool to reduce abortions?

Thanks to Michael New, Ph.D., economist and assistant professor at the University of Alabama, the answer is clear, and we also know where the *NY Times* went wrong in its analysis. The answer is that parental involvement laws *do* reduce teen abortion rates, by as much as 25% (Texas) and over 33% (Virginia and South Dakota). Where the *NY Times* went wrong: Staff writers looked at data from only 6 of the 12 states which passed parental involvement laws since the mid-1990s, and they obtained the data from state health departments (which even the authors admitted are an unreliable source). They also analyzed the percentage of pregnancies ending in abortion, rather than the percentage of teens having abortions. Because relatively few teens under 18 give birth each year, that ratio can fluctuate widely. The pregnancy-to-abortion ratio also fails to take into account the fact that parental involvement laws can discourage teen sexual activity, thereby reducing *both* pregnancies and abortions among teens. . . .

Court Battles Will Continue

As the last three decades have shown, it is not enough to have a majority pro-life citizenry, or even for state and federal legislators to enact scores of pro-life laws. Once the U.S. Supreme Court constitutionalized the abortion issue in 1973, the Court effectively took many questions relating to abortion out of the hands of the people and their elected representatives, leaving them little leeway in crafting restrictions. Even popular common-sense laws like those mandating parental involvement in minors' abortion decisions sometimes have been struck down or made unenforceable during years of challenges and frivolous appeals.

The pro-life movement is not the only group frustrated by abortion rulings. Lower court judges, too, have taken issue with the vagaries of the Supreme Court's abortion policy. . . .

Today, we have many reasons to hope that the structure of current abortion law will be shaken down to its rickety foundations.

Reason 1: Changes in the membership of the U.S. Supreme Court may lead the Court, at least incrementally, out of the morass that is current Court-made abortion law.

Reason 2: In a rare 9-0 decision in a case involving abortion, the Supreme Court ruled in *Ayotte v. Planned Parenthood of Northern New England* that lower courts may have gone too far in invalidating a parental involvement law in its entirety where it may have raised constitutional concerns only in narrow circumstances hypothetically affecting few women. The absence of a "health exception"—which would have allowed a minor to avoid parental notice *and* the judicial bypass procedure should she face a medical emergency—did not justify invalidating the entire New Hampshire statute. The Court sent the case back to the lower court to determine if the legislature intended to allow the statute to remain in effect with its supposedly unconstitutional applications enjoined or whether it intended no statute at all to one with a health exception. Although the Court did not explain how narrow a health exception may be (e.g., danger of bodily impairment vs. any factor affecting her "well-being") or what standard of review courts should apply in evaluating challenges to laws on abortion, the Court may have put an end to the practice of routinely rejecting abortion laws (even laws against grotesque partial-birth abortions) on the Ripley's-Believe-It-or-Not "fact" situations concocted by the abortion industry. . . .

Reason 3: As noted earlier, in *National Abortion Federation v. Gonzales*, decided January 31, 2006, the U.S. Court of Appeals for the Second Circuit struck down the federal Partial-Birth Abortion Ban Act in a 2-1 decision. But three noteworthy aspects of the decision give reason for hope. First, the final ruling was deferred pending briefs by the parties on the possible effect of *Ayotte* on the outcome. In other words, could enjoining supposedly unconstitutional applications relating to health save the statute? Second, Chief Justice [John M., Jr.] Walker's frank concurring opinion illuminates the Supreme Court's errors in *Stenberg v. Carhart* [2002, striking down Nebraska's ban on partial-birth abortion], pointing the way for some aspects of that decision to be reconsidered. Third, a dissent by Judge [Chester J.] Straub presents cogent reasons why the federal statute should be found constitutional notwithstanding the *Stenberg v. Carhart* precedent. The Supreme Court cannot fail to take notice of the rebuke and the sound reasoning in these opinions as they consider the pending case on partial-birth abortion.

Reason 4: On February 21, [2006,] the Supreme Court granted the government's request to review a decision of the Eighth Circuit Court of Appeals in another challenge to the Partial-Birth Abortion Ban Act, *Gonzales v. Carhart*. This Fall [2006], the Court will have the opportunity to end the repugnant practice of partial-birth abortion and begin to introduce some clarity and reason into abortion jurisprudence. Should Justice [Supreme Court] [Anthony] Kennedy rule consistent with the principles he expressed in his dissenting opinion in *Stenberg v. Carhart*, the outcome of *Gonzales v. Carhart* may be different.

Reason 5: On February 24, [2006,] the U.S. Court of Appeals for the Sixth Circuit ruled, in *Planned Parenthood Cincinnati Region v. Taft*, that a lower court erred in holding that federal law mandates the inclusion of a general health exception in every abortion law. The case challenged an Ohio law which requires abortion doctors to strictly follow the FDA [U.S. Food and Drug Administration] protocols in dispensing RU-486 for abortion. In particular, the FDA permits RU-486 abortions only through 49 days' gestation. The pill is much less effective and carries far greater health risks after this time period. But Planned Parenthood adopted an "off-label" use, permitting the pills to be taken up to 63 days' gestation. And while the Appeals Court accepted the lower court's (erroneous) factual record that an RU-486 abortion after 49 days may be a safer alternative to surgical abortion for some unidentified number of women, the Appeals Court asked the lower court to reconsider the case in light of its opinion and the *Ayotte* decision. Given the mounting FDA record of adverse events involving RU-486, and two more, recent, deaths of American women who took RU-486, the claim that this drug is safer than surgical abortion for some women between 49–63 days' gestation is implausible at best. Medical studies estimate that RU-486 results in ten times the fatalities to women, from infection alone, than surgical abortion in early pregnancy—and that was calculated before the most recent deaths.

Reason 6: On February 28, [2006,] the Supreme Court ended a 20-year travesty in which the National Organization for Women (NOW) and others tried to punish pro-life activist Joe Scheidler on the basis of federal laws against racketeering and extortion. They argued that abortion clinic protests and counseling were a form of racketeering activity, designed to obstruct the commerce of abortion clinics. They lost; those who demonstrate peacefully and counsel women outside clinics, and the women and children whose lives are saved, are the real winners.

After 33 years of "raw judicial power" depriving the most vulnerable Americans of all legal respect or protection, are we seeing the end of this regime of abortion on demand? Perhaps only the beginning of the end. The advent of a culture of life, where all the weak are protected and pregnant women are accepted and supported *with* their unborn children, may still seem a long journey. But we can be forgiven if we think we can detect the first hint of the dawn.

Abortion Is a Social Failure

Misty Mealey

Misty Mealey is a wife and mother of three children; she resides in Roanoke, Virginia.

In January 1973, the U.S. Supreme Court made abortion on demand the law of the land. With *Roe v. Wade*, the Court finally forced America to violate her founding commitment to "life, liberty and justice for all."

But why cling to abstract ideals such as the sanctity of life when abortion offers a pragmatic solution to our worst societal scourges? Abortion advocates assured us that easy access to abortion would mean "every child a wanted child," which would reduce child abuse. It would reduce crime, since those unwanted and impoverished children who often grow into criminals would never be born. It would protect vulnerable women from being butchered by untrained abortionists cashing in on their desperation. Widespread abortion could only lead to stronger women, stronger families and a stronger society, they promised.

So has abortion lived up to its promises? The answer is a resounding "no."

Abortions Do Not Result in a Better Society

With nearly 46 million "unwanted" children eliminated via abortion since 1973, we should have seen child abuse plummet. But that's not what has happened. In 2003, nearly 1 million children were victims of abuse and neglect, with experts estimating that three times that number were actually abused. Almost 1,500 children died of their injuries that year, according to the U.S. Department of Health and Human Services, which reports that all types of child abuse have increased since 1980. For some reason, the plan to reduce crime by eliminating the potential victims just didn't pan out.

Nor have we seen any positive impact on crime in general because of abortion. Interestingly, "progressive" states that legalized abortion prior to *Roe v. Wade* experienced consistently higher homicide rates nearly every year between 1976 and 1998, according to Yale University law professor John Lott and Australian economist John Whitley. Lott and Whitley found that legalizing abortion actually increased state murder rates by up to 7 percent. It seems that the plan to reduce crime by eliminating the potential perpetrators floundered, too.

Legal Abortions Threaten Women's Lives

And what about the women whose lives would be dramatically improved by abortion? How have they fared?

Contrary to the claims that thousands of women were dying from illegal abortion prior to *Roe v. Wade*, the American Medical Association reports that the figure for 1950 was actually 263, and that those numbers were even dropping, with 119 abortion-related deaths in 1970. Regardless, legal abortion was supposed to virtually eliminate the chance that a woman would be injured or killed during an abortion.

Legal abortion is actually the fifth leading cause of maternal death in the United States.

Today, however, providers who had great personal incentive to perform a medically competent abortion prior to *Roe v. Wade* now practice in medicine's most unregulated specialty. And no matter what happens, the abortionist can always count on an army of abortion advocates to stymie any attempts to raise the bar. In 1989, the *Miami Herald* ran a story about a local abortion clinic whose conditions were so heinous that one woman died and another was maimed. Abortion proponents admitted that they had known about the clinic's conditions but had remained silent for political reasons. According to pro-choice advocate Janis Compton-Carr, "In my gut, I am completely aghast at what goes on at that place. But I staunchly oppose anything that would correct this situation in law."

Not surprisingly, then, "complications following abortions performed in free-standing clinics is one of the most frequent gynecologic emergencies . . . encountered," according to an article that appeared in the *Journal of the American Medical Association* in February 1983. Legal abortion is actually the fifth leading cause of maternal death in the United States. So much for "safe," legal abortion.

Aftereffects of an Abortion

But at least abortion empowers women—or so they say. For a choice that's supposed to be so beneficial, it's strange that so many post-abortive women find the experience anything but positive. Numerous studies have shown that women who abort have an increased incidence of depression, anxiety and suicide. They are at greater risk for substance abuse and often engage in years of uncharacteristically self-destructive behavior after their abortions. Many of these women, who were once staunchly pro-choice, are now speaking out against abortion. It seems that this "empowering" experience really leaves the vast majority of women feeling powerless, abandoned and violated.

For more than three decades we've been told keeping abortion legal is both the logical and the compassionate choice for America. We've been asked to ignore the innumerable deaths of unborn, innocent children, not to mention their physically and emotionally maimed mothers, because there is just so much to gain with abortion on demand.

But given the overwhelming evidence of this social experiment's failure, abortion proponents need to stop hiding the truth and admit to what abortion really is—an empty promise that continues to choke the life out of our great nation.

CHAPTER 3

Should Women
Have Greater Access
to Abortion?

Chapter Preface

Lisa, a single 22-year-old restaurant manager, discovered that she was pregnant. Soon thereafter, she decided to have an abortion. The clinic in her area, however, located just 15 minutes away, had suddenly closed its doors. With just four abortion doctors left in the state of Missouri, Lisa was forced to drive eight hours away to the nearest clinic. She had to make the same trip again two weeks later for a follow-up visit. For many women today, access to abortion depends on where they live and how much money they have.

Missouri is one of many states that are working furiously to restrict access to abortion. It now has a law that allows civil suits to be brought against anyone who assists a teen in getting an abortion. Legislators are reviewing several proposals, including the protection of pharmacists who refuse to fill prescriptions for the morning-after pills, providing tax credits to centers that discourage women from getting abortions, and requiring that pain relief be given to fetuses 20 weeks or older during an abortion. Abortion proponents have cried foul, and the battle for access to abortion continues to blaze across the nation.

Currently, two classes of women in this country have less access to abortion than the rest of the women: One is federal employees, the other is women in the military. Federal employees' health insurance specifically exempts coverage for abortions, even though this option is available to most women in the private sector. Military women and their dependents banned from receiving abortions in military hospitals when they are stationed overseas, even if they are willing to pay for the procedure. One owner of an abortion clinic in the South would add a third class of women: Those who are poor. She states that "people with means and privilege can receive abortion care, but really, still poor women cannot." She contends that "the right to an abortion is meaningless if a woman can't get one."

Mississippi, too, is creating new laws that limit access to abortion. According to a survey by the Feminist Majority Foundation, out of 25 pharmacies in the city of Jackson, only two stock emergency contraception. One physician, Dr. Joseph Booker, has written several of these prescriptions, only to discover that his patients cannot find anyone to fill them. Mississippi's schools teach either abstinence or nothing at all. The state has the third highest teen pregnancy rate in the country and, according to the National Center for Children in Poverty, more than half of the state's children under the age of six live in poverty. Many license plates in the state have "Choose Life" signatures, and the state gives most of the money from these sales to Christian-run crisis pregnancy centers. These centers often lead patients to believe that they are abortion clinics; in reality, their aim is to dissuade women from getting an abortion, counsel against contraception, and propose abstinence as the only option for single women.

In light of abortion-limiting legislation and proponents who advocate greater access to abortion, the authors in the following chapter argue the merits of each position.

Women Need Greater Access to Abortion

Michelle Goldberg

Michelle Goldberg is a contributing writer to Salon.com and is the author of Kingdom Coming: The Rise of Christian Nationalism.

On Tuesday, July 18th, [2006,] for the first time in ten years, protestors arrived on Dr. Joseph Booker's block in Jackson, Mississippi. They went door to door, ringing bells and telling people that their neighbor, the state's last abortion provider, is a baby killer. A few weeks before that, protestors showed up at the Raleigh, North Carolina, home of Susan Hill, the owner of the Jackson Women's Health Organization, the clinic where Booker works. Soon the death threats started coming. "There is a feeling that things are ramping up," Hill says. "The protestors that we see in various places are more vocal, screaming, not just protesting." In her experience, clinic violence is often preceded by just this kind of heightened rhetoric.

The clinic's staff and most of the patients are black; the majority of the protestors are white.

The last abortion clinic in Mississippi is under siege. In mid-July [2006], Operation Save America—previously known as Operation Rescue—held a week of protests outside the Jackson Women's Health Organization. The next week, another anti-abortion group called Oh Saratoga! commenced its own seven days of demonstrations. Impatient for a change in

Michelle Goldberg, "Laying Siege to the Last Abortion Clinic in Mississippi," *The Public Eye Magazine*, fall 2006. Reproduced by permission of the author.

the Supreme Court, anti-abortion forces are determined to make *Roe v. Wade* functionally irrelevant in the state, and they believe they're getting close.

Protesters Aim to Shut Down Clinics

A decade ago, there were six clinics in Mississippi. Yet the combination of constant harassment and onerous regulations led one after another to shut down, and since 2004, Jackson Women's Health Organization has stood alone. Closing it would be the biggest victory yet in the anti-abortion movement's long war of attrition. This makes Mississippi an alluring target.

Hill owns five clinics throughout the country, and she has to be on constant alert. Over the years, her facilities have been subjected to 17 arsons or firebombings, as well as butyric acid attacks and anthrax threats. One of the doctors who was murdered, David Gunn, worked for her. "Fortunately we've been safer in the last few years for whatever reasons," says Hill. "Thank God there haven't been the shootings."

Race is an omnipresent issue at the protests, though it shows up in unexpected ways. The clinic's staff and most of the patients are black; the majority of the protestors are white. Still, the demonstrators see themselves as the heirs of the civil rights movement—they carry pictures of Martin Luther King, Jr., compare the pro-choice movement to the KKK [Ku Klux Klan] and call abortion "black genocide." What they generally refuse to do, though, is support government—measures that might ease the burdens of poverty in the state's poor, black communities—or help women better control their reproductive lives. Mississippi's high rate of unplanned pregnancies, says [antiabortion demonstrator C. Roy] McMillan, is due to the "moral degeneration of the black culture, and I submit it's caused by the welfare mentality."

Legislation Aimed at Closing Clinics

The protests are just one side of the vise that the Jackson Women's Health Organization and the women it serves are caught in. Both are also being squeezed by an ever-expanding panoply of anti-abortion legislation that's made Mississippi the most difficult state in America in which to terminate a pregnancy. Even as the Jackson Women's Health Organization hangs on, the state offers the country's clearest view of the religious Right's social agenda in action. It's a harbinger of what a post-*Roe* America could look like.

On July 19, [2006,] a white taxi that says "Choose Life" on its side pulled into the parking lot of the Jackson Women's Health Center. Out jumped one of the clinic's surgical technicians. Her boyfriend is a cab driver, and his boss, the owner of Veterans Taxi, has emblazoned the anti-abortion message on every car in his fleet. Opposition to abortion is everywhere in this state—more than an ideology, it's part of the atmosphere. Recently, Mississippi came close to following South Dakota and banning most abortions; many expect it will do so during the next legislative session. The local government leads the nation in anti-abortion legislation. Mississippi is one of only two states in America where teenagers seeking abortions need the consent of both parents, forcing some mothers to go to court to help their daughters override a father's veto.

Selective Reproductive Health Advice

Many cars have "Choose Life" license plates; the state gives much of the proceeds from the plates to Christian crisis pregnancy centers. More than two-dozen such centers operate in the state. They look very much like reproductive health clinics, and they offer free pregnancy tests and ultrasounds, but they exist primarily to dissuade women from having abortions. Like other crisis pregnancy centers nationwide, those in Mississippi tell their clients that abortion increases the risk of breast cancer, infertility and a host of psychiatric disorders, none of which is true. And although the women who come to them are virtually all both sexually active and unprepared for motherhood, they also counsel against contraception, believing that abstinence is the only answer for the unwed. At Jackson's Center for Pregnancy Choices, which gets around $20,000 a year in money from the Choose Life plates, a pamphlet about condoms warned, "[U]sing condoms is like playing Russian roulette. . . . In chamber one you have a condom that breaks and you get syphilis, in chamber two, you have an STD [sexually transmitted disease] that condoms don't protect against at all, in chamber three you have a routinely fatal disease, in chamber four you have a new STD that hasn't even been studied. . . ."

According to Barbara Beavers, a former sidewalk protestor who now runs the Center for Pregnancy Choices, as many as 40 percent of the pregnancy tests the center administer come back negative. Some of the women who take them live with their boyfriends, making a commitment to abstinence unlikely. But Beavers is unapologetic about her opposition to birth control, in part because she thinks a woman whose contraception fails might feel more entitled to an abortion. "They think, it wasn't their fault anyhow, so let's just go ahead and kill it," she says.

Already, places like the Center for Pregnancy Choices are leading public dispensers of reproductive health advice in Mississippi. The schools teach either abstinence or nothing at all. Besides private physicians, the only places that provide birth control prescriptions are the Jackson Women's Health Organization and the offices of the State Department of Health.

Hurdles and Enforced Ignorance

For women seeking to avoid pregnancy, there are other hurdles. According to a survey by the Feminist Majority Foundation, of 25 pharmacies in Jackson, only two stock emergency contraception (EC). Even when the pharmacies do carry EC, individual pharmacists may refuse to dispense it; Mississippi is one of eight states with "conscience clause" laws protecting pharmacists who refuse to dispense contraceptives. Dr. Booker says he has written several EC prescriptions, only to find his patients unable to fill them.

The number of abortion providers dropped 11 percent between 1996 and 2000, and almost 90 percent of U.S. counties lack abortion services.

Not surprisingly, Mississippi has the third highest teen pregnancy rate in the country, and the highest teenage birth rate. It is tied with Louisiana for America's worst infant mortality rate. According to The National Center for Children in Poverty, more than half of the state's children under 6 live in poverty. The immiseration of Mississippi's women and children isn't solely the result of diminished reproductive rights, of course. But it's clear that enforced ignorance and lack of choices play a major role. "You would be surprised what they don't understand about their own bodies," Betty Thompson, the former director of the Jackson Women's Health Organization, says about the clinic's patients.

Limitations Are Growing

For the anti-abortion movement, though, Mississippi isn't lagging behind the rest of the nation. Rather, it's the vanguard. "We're not waiting for the president, we're not waiting for the Congress, we're not waiting for the Supreme Court to be packed," says [Flip] Benham, the head of Operation Save America. "This issue can't be won from the top down. When you're on the streets and you see these battles won over and over again, when you see the statistics of abortion dropping, you begin to realize hey, this battle is being won."

Indeed, the same strategy at work in Mississippi is being used all across the country. According to the National Abortion Federation, 500 state-level anti-abortion bills were introduced last year, and 26 were signed into law. The number of abortion providers dropped 11 percent between 1996 and 2000, and almost 90 percent of U.S. counties lack abortion services.

Abortion rights won't disappear in America in one fell swoop, and they can't be protected by a single Supreme Court precedent. Congress's ban on adults taking a minor who is not their child across state lines for an abortion, and South Dakota's attempt to ban abortion outright, are making headlines. But the more gradual erosion of rights often escapes people's view. Through a combination of militant street actions and punitive legislation, *Roe v. Wade* is being hollowed out from the inside. The right to an abortion doesn't mean much if there's no way to get one.

Politicians Threaten
Access to Abortions

"Anonymous"

This anonymous viewpoint was submitted to the Progressive *for publication.*

Four days after his second inauguration, George [W.] Bush addressed an anti-abortion rally in Washington, D.C., by phone. "The America of our dreams, where every child is welcomed in law, in life, and protected in law, may be some ways away, but even from the far side of the river . . . we can see its glimmerings," he told the crowd. "I ask that God bless you for your dedication."

Senator Sam Brownback, Republican of Kansas, went even further. "The end of abortion on demand has started," he said to the tens of thousands of people who attended the rally. Interviewed by an anti-abortion group at the event, he also said, "This is a pro-life country."

If Bush and Brownback and the anti-abortion movement have their way, it will be, even though the majority of Americans support choice.

Politicians, Not Americans, Oppose Abortion

But the views of the public are not dominating the debate in Washington and in statehouses around the country. The views of the anti-abortion zealots are.

Even as many pro-choice people have been worrying about the potential calamity that awaits in the Supreme Court, the anti-abortion forces have been busy gaining ground elsewhere. The Bush Administration has promoted anti-abortion policies both internationally and domestically. Congress has more fanatical members than ever, none more so than newly elected Senator Tom Coburn, Republican of Oklahoma, who advocates the death penalty for doctors who provide abortions. And the action in the states is overwhelmingly hostile.

As a result, a woman in America today has far less freedom to have an abortion than a woman in America the day after *Roe v. Wade* was handed down in 1973. And for poor women, who are disproportionately of color, that freedom is hanging by a thread.

When Bush submitted his $2.57 trillion budget, he once again failed to provide a single penny to the United Nations [UN] Population Fund, which provides more assistance to women in the Third World than any other group.

This global gag rule is not making abortions rarer. It's just making them more dangerous.

"The Administration is implementing a stealth campaign to limit women's health programs around the world because they include reproductive health," says Anika Rahman, president of the U.S. Committee for the U.N. Population Fund. "Women's health programs, especially those that provide women with voluntary family planning services, elevate the status of women in their societies, and lead to economic development."

Rahman's group noted that Congress had allocated $34 million this year [2005] for the fund, which "could prevent the deaths of 4,700 women who die during childbirth from preventable causes and 77,000 infants and young children who die because their mothers aren't healthy enough to breast feed." And the irony is that these funds could also "prevent two million unplanned and unwanted pregnancies that result in 800,000 abortions annually." But Bush continues to refuse to release the money.

In addition, Bush is maintaining the "global gag rule," which denies overseas family planning organizations any U.S. aid if they even provide abortion counseling or referrals. "The global gag rule therefore forces a cruel choice: In starkest terms, foreign NGOs (nongovernmental organizations) can either choose to accept USAID [U.S. Agency for International Development] funds for provision of essential health services—but with restrictions which may jeopardize the health of many patients—or the NGOs can choose to reject the policy and lose vital U.S. support," says the Global Gag Rule Impact Project, run by pro-choice groups. "In a number of countries, established referral networks of providers are collapsing as leading family planning NGOs downsize and struggle to cope with budget cuts and rapidly declining stocks of contraceptive supplies."

This global gag rule is not making abortions rarer. It's just making them more dangerous. "Of the forty-six million abortions that occur each year, roughly twenty million are performed under unsafe conditions," according to Planned Parenthood. "Each year, an estimated 80,000 women die from complications of unsafe abortions." According to the World Health Organization, 95 percent of unsafe abortions take place in the Third World.

Politicians Play Doctor

In domestic policy, Bush and the Republicans are picking up where they left off in November, when they rammed through a law that allows for-profit hospitals, HMOs, and other health care companies receiving federal funds to bar their physicians from even discussing abortion with their patients. And it penalizes states or local governments that would require these health care companies to offer abortions, counseling, or referrals.

Senate Majority Leader Bill Frist has said that one of his top ten legislative priorities is the "Child Custody Protection

Act [this legislation passed on January 24, 2005]." It . . . pro-hibit[s] anyone except a parent from transporting a minor across state lines for an abortion unless the minor had ful-filled whatever parental notification law may be in effect in her state. More than thirty states have such laws. The penalty for violating this law is up to a year in prison. The only excep-tion is "if the abortion was necessary to save the life of the minor because her life was endangered by a physical disorder, physical injury, or physical illness." Anti-abortion groups be-lieve they can pass this into law this year.

And Bush's answer to unwanted pregnancies is simply more money for abstinence only.

Then there is the "Federal Unborn Child Pain Awareness Act [passed on September 19, 2006]." Introduced by Brown-back and Representative Chris Smith, Republican of New Jer-sey, this bill . . . require[s] abortion providers to tell any woman seeking an abortion past the twentieth week that the fetus would be experiencing pain during the abortion. The bill even provides the actual wording that the provider must de-liver verbally. "The Congress of the United States has deter-mined that at this stage of development, an unborn child has the physical structures necessary to experience pain," it states. "Congress finds that there is substantial evidence that the pro-cess of being killed in an abortion will cause the unborn child pain." And it also requires the provider to tell the woman that she has "the option of choosing to have anesthesia or other pain reducing drug or drugs administered directly to the pain-capable unborn child." The script adds: "In some cases, there may be some additional risk to you associated with adminis-tering such a drug."

More inventive is the "Informed Choice Act" [still pending in the House in 2007], introduced by Representative Cliff Stearns, Republican of Florida. It would allow the Department of Health and Human Services to give grants for ultrasound equipment to nonprofit community-based pregnancy [health] medical clinics. In exchange for receiving the grant, the clinic would have to show "the visual image of the fetus" to the pregnant woman and provide her with "information on abortion and alternatives to abortion such as childbirth and adoption and information concerning public and private agencies that will assist in those alternatives."

Everything they do now is a movement to give personhood to a fetus.

Meanwhile, as Republicans are thinking of evermore ingenious ways to restrict the right to an abortion, Bush himself is cutting back on Medicaid funds so that facilities which treat the poor have a harder time doing so. And Bush's answer to unwanted pregnancies is simply more money for abstinence only. He is advocating such a move even though some federally funded abstinence-only programs have spread ridiculous information, such as that touching a person's genitals "can result in pregnancy," as a report by Representative Henry Waxman, Democrat of California, revealed.

Numerous States Aim to Circumvent Abortion Rights

The anti-abortion campaigns at the state level are galloping along, even in places you might not expect, like Michigan, which went to John Kerry and has a pro-choice governor, Jennifer Granholm. Michigan got an F on a recent report card made out by NARAL [National Abortion and Reproductive Rights Action League] Pro-Choice America. The state ranked forty-fifth, according to the group.

One reason for Michigan's slide is that the state adopted a law last year [2004] that defines a fetus as a "legally born person" when any part of the fetus is outside the woman's body and shows signs of life. Ostensibly designed to outlaw so-called partial birth abortions, the law, which is slated to take effect at the end of March [2005], does not stop there.

State legislatures considered more than 500 antichoice bills in 2004, according to the National Abortion Federation.

"This radical law goes far beyond any other legislation in the country, threatening women's ability to obtain even a first-trimester abortion and, in some instances, preventing doctors from treating miscarriages," said the Reverend Mark Pawlowski, CEO of Planned Parenthood of South Central Michigan. Planned Parenthood, along with the ACLU [American Civil Liberties Union] and the Center for Reproductive Rights, is suing in federal court to try to stop the law.

According to those groups, "a doctor would be unable to provide a woman with an abortion even if she suffers from diabetes or cardiac ailments and needs an abortion to protect her health."

The Michigan anti-abortion legislators aren't satisfied yet. "One bill they've put in is to allow for a federal tax deduction for a still-born birth," says Shelli Weisberg, a lobbyist for the Michigan ACLU. "Everything they do now is a movement to give personhood to a fetus. They come up with amazing things."

State legislatures considered more than 500 anti-choice bills in 2004, according to the National Abortion Federation. These proposed restrictions included abortion bans, parental notifications, antiabortion counseling, waiting periods, and the imposition of burdensome regulations on abortion clinics, such as specifications for the widths of doorways.

Mississippi is one of the more difficult places to get an abortion. It is the only state whose Democratic Party platform opposes a woman's right to choose. Only one abortion clinic serves the entire state. And the state legislature has placed a slew of restrictions on women seeking abortions.

Lies, Restrictions, and Obstacles

Mississippi is one of two states that require the consent of both parents before a minor can get an abortion. And it joins Texas in demanding that women be told that having an abortion increases the threat of breast cancer, even though the National Cancer Institute does not support that claim.

Mississippi enacted a law in 2004 that requires abortions after the first trimester be performed in a hospital. The law effectively bans second trimester abortions, as no hospitals in the state perform the procedure after sixteen weeks. Litigation is so far blocking the enforcement of this law. (Nationwide, 93 percent of abortions are performed in clinics, not hospitals, according to the Alan Guttmacher Institute.)

In May 2004, Mississippi's legislature passed the single most expansive refusal law in the nation. Also known as a "conscience clause," the law allows any health care provider to refuse to be involved in any service—from referrals to abortions—they object to on moral, ethical, or religious grounds. "Forty-six states allow some health care providers to refuse to provide abortion services," the Guttmacher Institute says.

Texas and Utah require parental consent for adolescents who seek state-funded family planning services. Several states, including Kentucky, Minnesota, and Virginia, introduced bills last year [2004] that would impose new requirements for parental consent for teens wanting contraception.

West Virginia is of concern to pro-choice activists, if only because of the sheer number of bills introduced. More than thirty that limit a woman's right to choose are circulating in that legislature.

Kansas's Attorney General Phill Kline is demanding that abortion clinics turn over the complete medical records— including the patient's name, medical history, details of her sex life, birth control practices, and psychological profile—of ninety females who had late-term abortions. Kline, who is anti-abortion, first said he was looking for cases of underage victims of rape. A week later he acknowledged that his investigation is also aimed at "criminal late-term abortion."

This case echoes [former U.S. Attorney General] John Ashcroft's 2004 subpoena of the medical records of 900 women who sought abortions at six Planned Parenthood clinics across the country. Three federal district courts declared Ashcroft's demand unconstitutional.

Voters Need to Fight Back

For too long, we've worried too much about the Supreme Court. Not that it isn't vitally important, but our ability as citizens to affect that outcome is weak, and the timing of such work is intermittent. We can vote for a President who we believe will appoint justices who will uphold the right to choose. We can vote for Senators who we trust will oppose anti-choice nominees. And we can lobby our Senators when the nominations come down.

But between those events, we cannot rest.

We need, on a daily basis, to convince our fellow citizens of the importance of this right. And we need, at the state level, to pressure our local legislators to heed the views of a majority of Americans, a majority that still believes in the right to choose.

Late-Term Abortions Should Not Be Banned

Jason Abaluck

Jason Abaluck is the president of Perspective, Harvard Liberal Monthly Magazine, *at Harvard University.*

When asked whether abortion should be legal, 80 percent of Americans say yes. When asked the same question about so-called "partial-birth abortion," 20 percent say yes. This dramatic difference reflects in part the important role that terminology has played in the abortion debate. From the dueling labels "pro-life" and "pro-choice" to a recent Missouri law that attempted to rename abortion as "infanticide," both sides have understandably attempted to cast their views in the most appealing light. In this case, the anti-abortion lobby seems to have won the label war; it isn't particularly surprising that most people oppose "partial-birth abortion" since the term suggests that the procedure is equivalent to killing a fully developed baby.

Ignoring briefly the effects of terminology, it is not inherently inconsistent to permit some but not all abortions. For the 80 percent of Americans who recognize that the mother's fundamental liberty to determine the course of her life outweighs the rights of an embryo—but presumably believe it is wrong for a mother to kill her newborn baby—a line must be drawn somewhere. This line, however, must be drawn in a logical and consistent way and without infringing unnecessarily on a woman's rights. In evaluating the recently [2003] passed ban on partial-birth abortion, then, we must consider two questions: first, is the D & X (dilation and extraction) procedure—the medical procedure generally equated to a

Jason Abaluck, "Partial Truths: The Partial-birth Abortion Ban Violates Women's Rights," *Perspective, Harvard Liberal Monthly Magazine*, November 2003. Reproduced by permission.

"partial-birth abortion"—a reasonable place to draw that line? Second, does the partial-birth ban draw that line consistently? The answer to both of these questions is a definite "no." Given this reality, it is impossible to ignore what is actually at stake in the recent ban. [The U.S. Supreme Court heard arguments on November 8, 2006, to overrule the ban.]

Politicians Claim Women Safety Concerns

First, it is important to examine [the] claim that the partial-birth ban is designed to protect the interests of the mother. According to the bill recently passed by Congress, "a ban on partial birth abortion will . . . advance the health interests of pregnant women seeking to terminate a pregnancy." The bill states that there is "no credible medical evidence that partial-birth abortions are safe or are safer than other abortion procedures. . . . A ban on partial-birth abortion is not required to contain a 'health' exception, because the facts indicate that a partial-birth abortion is never necessary to preserve the health of a woman."

The American College of Obstetricians and Gynecologists . . . opposes attempts to ban "partial-birth" abortions as 'inapropriate, ill advised, and dangerous.'

As the Supreme Court observed when it last invalidated a ban on the D & X procedure in *Stenberg v. Carhart* (2000), there is considerable controversy within the medical community as to whether D & X is in fact safer than its alternatives. The controversy is by no means settled today, in the sense that there have been no conclusive studies demonstrating that the D & X procedure is safer or less safe than other available techniques. Yet it is difficult to understand why this would be a contentious issue at all if no one believed that D & X was safer in some circumstances. Why would women and their doctors ever choose a procedure that they believe to be more dangerous than the alternatives? The D & X procedure is not easier or less costly to perform than the alternatives. On almost no other issues does Congress pretend to know more about medicine than medical doctors—and this presumption is especially inappropriate for such a politically charged issue. As Justice [Stephen] Breyer wrote in the *Stenberg* majority opinion, "Where a significant body of medical opinion believes a procedure may bring with it greater safety for some patients and explains the medical reasons supporting that view, (the Court) cannot say that the presence of a different view by itself proves the contrary." Indeed, the American College of Obstetricians and Gynecologists, which accounts for over 95 percent of board-certified obstetricians and gynecologists in the United States, opposes attempts to ban "partial birth" abortions as "inappropriate, ill advised, and dangerous."

The Supreme Court has repeatedly affirmed that a woman has the right to terminate her pregnancy before viability.

Lawmakers Aim to Protect Fetuses, Not Women

These facts make the bill's claim that the D & X procedure is never the best choice for women and its lack of a health exception for the mother particularly suspect. Why would Congress use this reasoning, knowing full well that the Supreme Court should rule it unconstitutional as they did in *Stenberg v. Carhart*? What harm would be done by including a health exception if, by Congress's own contention, it would never be exercised? From this, it is evident that this bill is not designed to serve the interests of pregnant mothers. Some insight into actual motives for the bill can be gained by noting its chief sponsor—Pennsylvania Senator Rick Santorum. Notorious for comparing homosexuality to incest, bestiality, and adultery, Rick Santorum is not concerned with protecting the interests of pregnant women. He has clearly and emphatically stated that his goal is to ban abortion entirely. By failing to include an exception for the mother's health, Santorum and his ilk can make clear to their constituency that their concern is not with protecting women but with protecting fetuses.

For the sake of argument, let us assume that the bill did in fact contain an exception for the mother's health. Would it then establish clear and justifiable conditions under which the mother's liberty may be restricted for the sake of the fetus? To answer this question, we must first understand exactly what the procedure in question is. Partial-birth abortion refers, albeit vaguely and incorrectly, to a particular type of abortion known as D & X. ("Partial birth" itself is simply not a medical term.) D & X is a specific type of the more common dilation and evacuation procedure, also called D & E. In a D & E procedure, the most common type of abortion performed in the second trimester, the cervix is dilated and fetal tissue is removed surgically through the cervix. In the D & X procedure, however, the fetus is removed through the cervix intact. In a head-first presentation, the skull is collapsed and the entire fetus is extracted through the cervix; in the feet-first presentation, the body of the fetus is pulled through the cervix and the skull is collapsed and extracted.

Stenberg v. Carhart invalidated an earlier attempt to ban partial-birth abortions because the language of the bill was broad enough to be construed as a ban on D & E as well as D & X. The Supreme Court has repeatedly affirmed that a woman has the right to terminate her pregnancy before viability. Because D & E is the most common form of second trimester abortion, the bill would have severely restricted a woman's access to abortion at a stage of pregnancy before the fetus is viable and was thus unconstitutional. The congressional bill does alter the language explicitly deemed objectionable by the Supreme Court, but there is still controversy over whether the new language might be construed as a ban on some D & E procedures.

A Fetus Cannot Override a Woman's Rights

According to the bill, what is the relevant moral distinction between a fetus that is permissible to abort and a fetus whose rights override the claims of the mother? It cannot be fetal viability. While the precise definition of viability is controversial, both sides agree that the banned D & X procedure is performed both pre- and post-viability. Other variants of the D & E procedure, which the bill does not ban according to our assumption, are sometimes performed later in the development of the fetus than the D & X procedure. The only distinction seems to be that in the D & X procedure, either the fetal head or torso is outside the mother's body before the fetus is terminated. Is this a reasonable standard? According to this standard, we admit that the mother's right to liberty outweighs any claims of the fetus while the fetus is entirely within her body. It amounts to saying that the mother may not choose what is at least arguably the safest method of abortion if this option happens to involve moving the fetus a few inches in one direction.

Those who voted for it [the abortion ban] likely know it is unconstitutional.

One might argue that the mother's claims arise from the fact that the fetus is a part of her body, and that once part of the fetus is outside her body this is no longer true. In the D & X procedure, in contrast to the still-legal D & E procedure, the fetus is terminated outside the uterus. Still, at the time when a fetus is terminated in the D & X procedure, it is part of the mother in the most important sense—it cannot be extracted through the cervix in a way that is safe for the mother without being destroyed. The head is outside the uterus, but this does not seem like a morally relevant fact. Many doctors believe that this method avoids several risks involved with terminating the fetus inside the uterus. The whole reason for fetal termination is to ensure that the fetus can be removed without doing harm to the mother. If a mother has a right to choose abortion in the first place, she has a right to choose the safest method regardless of whether the fetus is terminated inside or outside the uterus.

Abortion Limits Are a Step toward Elimination of Abortion Rights

The abortion ban passed by Congress is certainly not for the benefit of women, and it fails to establish a reasonable standard to distinguish between permissible and impermissible abortions. Those who voted for it likely know it is unconstitutional, considering the similarities between the congressional law and the law invalidated by the Supreme Court in *Stenberg v. Carhart*. These supporters can be separated into two camps. On the one hand are those who oppose all abortion in principle and seek to make abortion less acceptable—and eventually, illegal—through an explicit strategy of incrementalism. For them, the ban on partial-birth abortion is just the next step after parental consent requirements and forced waiting periods toward repealing *Roe v. Wade*. Other supporters are moderate Republicans and Democrats who support *Roe v. Wade* but believe late-term abortions are wrong. For the reasons given above, it is difficult to believe that they agree with all the details of the current ban, but they are willing to bear its inadequacies in order to take a consistent stand against late-term abortions.

There is the danger that the moderates' willingness to compromise will aid the incrementalists' design. The danger is not a shift in public opinion. Polls show that Americans' feelings on the permissibility of abortion have not changed much in the past 25 years. Most Americans favor some limits on abortion, and a well-run public relations campaign that depends as much on terminology as substance has led most Americans to oppose partial-birth abortions. Barring some dramatic shift in the makeup of the Supreme Court, the Court will most likely find the partial-birth abortion ban unconstitutional. The real danger is subtler; the incrementalists could achieve their aim if those who support abortion become complacent and those who oppose it are galvanized. In such an environment, it would be politically feasible for a pro-life president, particularly one in his second term, to appoint justices who oppose *Roe v. Wade.* Those who support abortion rights must remain vigilant—because Congress and the President surely do not have women's best interests at heart.

We Should Strive to Reduce the Number of Abortions

Jessica Arons and Shira Saperstein

Jessica Arons is a legal policy associate for the Women's Health Project and the Faith and Progressive Policy Initiative at the Center for American Progress. Shira Saperstein is a senior fellow at the Center for American Progress and deputy director of the Moriah Fund.

Over the last year [2005], many moderate and progressive politicians have begun to voice a fairly consistent message about abortion. Wanting to distance themselves from the stereotype that the "Pro-Choice" position equals "abortion on demand," they have put forth a so-called moderate, "compromise" position: maintain *Roe v. Wade* but work to reduce the number of abortions in this country. At a rate of more than 1 million a year, reducing the annual number of abortions is certainly an admirable goal. However, there are different ways to reach that goal—some of which will help women and some of which will not.

Simply put, there are two key ways to reduce abortion—by making it less necessary or by making it less available. In our view, only the former approach is humane, effective, and just.

Anti-abortion Tactics Are Cruel, Hurtful, and Ineffective

Those who oppose abortion in all or most circumstances generally think the best way to reduce the number of abortions is to make it illegal. By eliminating legal availability, they believe abortion will cease to exist. They hold this view despite undeniable evidence that women continue to have abortions in

Jessica Arons and Shira Saperstein, "The Right Way to Reduce Abortion," American progress.org, January 20, 2006. This material was created by the Center for American Progress, www.americanprogress.org.

countries where it is outlawed, under illegal and unsafe conditions that often result in terrible tragedy. Close to 70,000 women a year die from unsafe abortion and numerous others suffer grave injuries, including infection, hemorrhaging, and infertility. This hurts women, their families, and whole communities, but it does very little to reduce abortion.

Making abortion less necessary is by far the better approach.

Anti-abortion advocates have not yet been able to achieve an outright ban on abortion in the United States. Thus, they have worked—very successfully—to make it as inaccessible as possible. By barring public funding, increasing the cost with unnecessary clinic regulations, decreasing the number of available doctors and clinics, imposing waiting periods, and mandating rigid parental involvement laws, anti-abortion activists have put safe and legal abortion completely beyond the reach of a significant segment of our population, namely the young, the rural, and most of all, the poor. As a result, many of the women who have been denied *Roe*'s protections have either carried and borne children against their will or have faced significant delay in obtaining an abortion, thereby making the procedure more costly, more risky, and more emotionally and morally challenging. Although the strategy of making abortion unavailable may reduce the number of abortions, it does so in a cruel and unacceptable way.

Education and Funding Key to Reducing Unintended Pregnancies

Making abortion less necessary is by far the better approach. The first way to do so is to reduce the incidence of unintended pregnancy. Half of all pregnancies in this country are unintended, and, of those, half end in abortion. Unintended pregnancy could be reduced significantly if we showed true commitment to: 1) comprehensive sexuality education that includes medically accurate information about abstinence *and* contraception; 2) insurance coverage of, and public funding for, family planning services; 3) greater access to emergency contraception (which prevents pregnancy and does not cause abortion); and 4) programs that curb domestic violence and sexual abuse. Clearly, women who are able to avoid unintended pregnancy do not have to make the difficult decision of whether to have an abortion.

Unfortunately, even with the supports listed above, there will always be some unintended pregnancies; birth control methods are fallible, as are human beings. Therefore, once a woman finds herself with an unexpected pregnancy, a second positive way to reduce abortion is to ensure that she has the means to have and raise a child in health and safety should she wish to do so. According to the Alan Guttmacher Institute, one of the two most common reasons women choose abortion is because they cannot afford another child. By providing low-income and young women with genuine education and career opportunities, health care, child care, housing, services for disabled children, and other basic supports, many would have the resources they need to fulfill the serious obligations that parenting brings.

Ineffecient Remedies Are Ineffective

Regrettably, few of these policy goals are mentioned in today's rhetoric about reducing abortion. Instead, the formula that many moderate politicians have adopted is to look at the list of restrictions promoted by anti-abortion activists—e.g., biased counseling, bans on public funding, prohibitions on specific abortion procedures—and "split the difference," supporting some, but not all, of them. Even the 95-10 initiative promoted by Democrats for Life, an ostensibly middle-of-the-road group that claims to have an agenda that would reduce abortions by 95 percent in 10 years, contains meager supports for pregnant women (funding for domestic violence programs and university day care), no provision for birth control, and only vague allusions to pregnancy prevention education.

These half-hearted approaches to abortion reduction are categorically insufficient and appear, more often than not, to reflect a watered down "Pro-Life" agenda rather than a genuine moderate, let alone progressive, one.

Moderation for its own sake and political compromise that sacrifices women's well-being will not achieve the common goal of reducing abortion in this country. What is needed is leadership and commitment to a vision of society in which *all* women have the information and means necessary to prevent unintended pregnancies, to carry healthy pregnancies to term, to raise their children with safety, stability, and dignity, and, yes, to have safe abortions when necessary to lead healthy, productive, and fulfilling lives.

Birth Control Methods Are Another Form of Abortion That Needs to Be Eliminated

Life and Liberty Ministries

In 1993 Denny Green moved to Virginia to begin Life and Liberty Ministries. In July 1994 he officially opened a maternity home and began daily street outreach at Richmond area abortion clinics.

Did you know that many commonly used forms of "birth control" or "contraception" can actually cause an abortion early in a pregnancy? It's true.

Some methods of "family planning" should give Christians cause to reconsider. Facts concerning the mechanisms through which most methods of "contraception" prevent the birth of a baby are enough to establish that there are grave moral problems that arise.

Do not be fooled into dismissing concerns over "birth control" as simply a "Catholic issue." It is worth noting that remarkable church leaders like Martin Luther, John Calvin, and John Wesley criticized practices aimed at preventing or terminating a pregnancy.

IUDs Do Not Prevent Conception

The average person has little knowledge of the way various birth control methods such as the Pill, Depo-Provera, Norplant, and the intrauterine device (IUD) work. Take a moment to read some of the facts concerning the most popular methods used to avoid having a baby.

The intrauterine device, or IUD is not a contraceptive. That is, it does not prevent fertilization, the joining of an egg

Life and Liberty Ministries, "The Pill Kills Babies," www.lifeandlibertyministries.com, August 1, 2004. Reproduced by permission.

and sperm, from occurring (conception). It does nothing to disrupt ovulation, the menstrual cycle, or to thicken the cervical mucous.

The IUD is a device which is inserted into the womb and which creates a hostile environment by irritating and thinning the endometrium, the lining of the uterus. Such a state of irritation leaves the uterine wall unprepared for the process of implantation when a newly conceived baby attempts to cleave to the wall of the uterus.

Though literature on the IUD suggests that perhaps fertilization may be prevented, that perhaps copper in the IUD kills sperm, there is no evidence to support the hypothesis that sperm are killed or that fertilization is prevented at all. In fact, G.D. Searle, one company that produces the IUD, conceded early on that the device does nothing more than prevent the unborn child from attaching to the wall of the uterus:

> The action of the IUDs would seem to be a simple local phenomenon. That these devices prevent nidation implantation of an already fertilized ovum has been accepted as the most likely mechanism of action.

So, when the conceived child, driven by nature, seeks out the warmth, nutrition, and comfort of the mother's womb, the IUD has essentially put out an "Unwelcome" mat.

Understanding that human life begins at conception, this intentional disruption of the uterine environment produces an early abortion. The unborn child, unable to implant, starves for lack of nutrition, dies, and is sloughed off during the next menstrual cycle.

Chemicals Destroy Fertilized Eggs

RU-486 is an anti-progesterone, but some birth control falls into the category of progesterones which can be delivered orally, vaginally or by injection. A common one is Depo-Provera (DMPA).

This drug is generally administered by injection intramuscularly every three months. It is thought that by inhibiting the secretion of pituitary gonadotropin, DMPA acts to suppress ovulation. It also irritates and thins the lining of the uterus, making implantation of the newly conceived person unlikely. DMPA is recommended for use as a contraceptive by its manufacturer, Upjohn.

Norplant, too, is a progesterone drug which is increasingly popular despite significant risks which are associated with it. The drug is encased in five or six flexible closed capsules, or rods, which are surgically implanted beneath the skin.

Again, pregnancy is either avoided through the suppression of ovulation, or, should ovulation occur, an irritation to the uterine wall prevents placental implantation of the child.

The Pill is called an oral contraceptive, implying that conception is prevented. However, actual prevention of pregnancy is only true for two of its three mechanisms. The three mechanisms are briefly indicated in this quote from the *Physician's Desk Reference*:

> Although the primary mechanism of this action is inhibition of ovulation, other alterations in the genital tract, including changes in the cervical mucous (which increase the difficulty of sperm entry into the uterus) and the endometrium (which may reduce the likelihood of implantation) may also contribute to contraceptive effectiveness.

Calling these methods 'contraceptive' is deceptive.

So, to summarize, the mechanisms by which the Pill can prevent the birth of a baby are:

- inhibiting ovulation, and thus preventing fertilization from ever occurring.

- thickening the cervical mucous, thereby making it more difficult for sperm cells to travel into the uterus, and reducing the chance that fertilization might occur.

But should there be what the medical literature refers to as a "breakthrough ovulation" (a failure to prevent ovulation) and a resulting pregnancy (fertilization), the Pill also performs a function similar to the IUD. The Pill, too, provides a chemical mechanism which makes the uterus a hostile environment by changing the endometrium, thinning it, so that implantation does not occur. The unborn child is aborted.

We must not compromise by refusing to address methods of birth control which result in an abortion.

In the end, it does exactly the same work as the much publicized abortion pill, RU-486. This information is not new, and the disruption that causes early chemical abortion is not limited to a few types of the Pills. With all of the oral contraceptives, it is estimated that the abortion-causing mechanism comes into play between 2% and 10% of the time. In fact, the "mini-pills," which have no estrogen, allow ovulation to take place 40–60% of the time. Still, drug companies elect to call their products "contraceptive."

Contraception Deception

Calling these methods "contraceptive" is deceptive. Such deception has meant that many Christians who would not ever consider terminating a pregnancy through one of the methods of surgical abortion are unknowingly using methods of birth control which, at least 2% to 10% of the time, may be taking the life of a newly conceived child.

Dr. Bogomir Kuhar, a pharmacist and expert on chemical abortion, has calculated that combining all forms of nonsurgical induced abortion—IUD, injections like Depo-Provera, implants such as Norplant, and the Pill—between 8 [million] and 12 million young lives are killed in the United States each year through these chemicals and devices.

Many people have wondered why the church has seemed to have so little effect when it comes to stopping legal abortion in America. Is it possible that, knowingly or unknowingly, "contraceptive" practices used by Christians have robbed the church of her moral authority to speak against abortion?

When we, as Christians, declare the biblical truth that human life begins at conception, and that we oppose abortion, we must be consistent. We must not compromise by refusing to address methods of birth control which result in an abortion. Not only are we accountable for applying truth in our own lives, as Christian counselors and leaders, we need to share what we know.

We need to stop promoting the world's view of "family planning." Our pre-marital counseling should address the abortion risk inherent in these popular methods of birth control. Christian couples are entitled to know that some methods of birth control can be deadly for their unborn children.

Partial-Birth Abortions Should Be Banned

Rich Deem

Rich Deem has worked in basic science research since 1976. He has authored and coauthored a number of studies, and is employed as a researcher/specialist, at Cedars-Sinai Medical Center in the Inflamatory Bowel Disease Center.

A kind of late-term abortion, D&X (also known as partial birth abortion) has been in the news for several years. Many states have passed legislation banning this procedure because of its immoral nature. The Congress has also passed legislation to ban the procedure, all of which have been vetoed by President [Bill] Clinton. A description of the procedure and why it is *never* medically necessary follows. **Warning**: the description below is graphic and upsetting to most people. Do not continue if you are unwilling to suffer some emotional trauma.

Viable Fetuses Are Killed

Where is the most dangerous place in the United States? Contrary to what most people might think, it is not the inner city, or even death row in many states. The most dangerous place to be in the United States is in the womb of our nation's women. One out of three pregnancies is terminated (the fetus is killed) by the mother. In other nations, the death toll is even higher. For example, over 70% of all pregnancies in Russia are terminated through abortion. Proponents of abortion want it to be "safe and rare," something it has never been. More than 95% of all abortions are performed purely for convenience (i.e., not using birth control). However upsetting these statistics may be, they seem mild to the reality of late-

Rich Deem, "D&X (Partial Birth) Abortions," www.godandscience.org, April 11, 2006. Reproduced by permission.

term abortions, performed on tens of thousands of viable fetuses every year. Babies often survive the procedure to be born alive. . . . However, since they are unwanted, they are left alone to die—a process that often takes many hours. . . .

This procedure is closer to infanticide than it is to abortion.

The D&X procedure itself is rather gruesome. The abortion practitioner instrumentally reaches into the uterus, grasps the fetus' feet, and pulls the feet down into the cervix. The reason this is done is not as a medical necessity, but to avoid actually birthing the baby. If the baby were fully born, killing it would be considered murder. The fetus is then pulled down the birth canal until it has been entirely birthed except the head. Surgical scissors are forced into the base of the fetal skull while the fetus is lodged in the birth canal. This blind procedure risks maternal injury from laceration of the uterus or cervix by the scissors and could result in severe bleeding and the threat of shock or even maternal death. A suction apparatus is introduced into the hole in the base of the skull and the fetus' brains are removed through aspiration. The baby is then born dead. The entire procedure is performed on the fetus without the use of anesthesia even though it is clearly capable of feeling pain (studies have shown that the ability to feel pain begins early in the second trimester).

D&X Is Risky and Needless

D&X is most commonly performed between 20 and 24 weeks and thereby raises questions of the potential viability of the fetus. Information from 1988 through 1991 indicates a 15% viability rate at 23 weeks gestation, 56% at 24 weeks, and 79% at 25 weeks. Proponents of D&X have asserted that the procedure was rarely performed (approximately 450–500 per year) and only used in extreme cases when a woman's life was at risk or the fetus had a condition incompatible with life. In actuality, one facility alone admitted to performing 1,500 of these procedures, the vast majority of which were carried out on healthy mothers with normal fetuses. Dayton, Ohio, physician Martin Haskell, MD, who had performed more than 700 partial-birth abortions, stated that most of his abortions are elective in that 20- to 24-week range and that "probably 20% are for genetic reasons, and the other 80% are purely elective." James T. McMahon, MD, of Los Angeles, CA, in detailing for the US Congress his experience with more than 2,000 partial-birth abortion procedures stated that only 9% of those involved maternal health indications (of which the most common was depression). In fact, the insertion of instruments into the uterus is not without risks, since 1 out of 6,000 of these kinds of procedures results in the death of the mother (death from childbirth is 1 out of 13,000). Is the procedure ever medically necessary? First of all, the procedure itself requires several days to perform, since the cervix must be dilated first. This means that the procedure is *never* used in an emergency to save the life of the mother. In addition, the procedure is medically risky to the mother. According to Drs. M. LeRoy Sprang and Mark G. Neerhof:

> None of these risks are medically necessary because other procedures are available to physicians who deem it necessary to perform an abortion late in pregnancy. As ACOG policy states clearly, intact D&X is never the only procedure available.

In writing for the *Journal of the American Medical Association*, Drs. M. LeRoy Sprang and Mark G. Neerhof, conclude with the following statement:

> Intact D&X (partial-birth abortion) should not be performed because it is needlessly risky, inhumane, and ethically unacceptable. This procedure is closer to infanticide than it is to abortion.

CHAPTER 4

Should Protesters Target Abortion Clinics and Providers?

Chapter Preface

On February 28, 2006, the U.S. Supreme Court ended a 20-year battle by ruling that the Hobbs Act and federal extortion and racketeering laws cannot be used against anti-abortion demonstrators. The legal cases of *Scheidler et al. v. National Organization for Women, Inc., et al.*, and *Operation Rescue v. National Organization for Women, Inc., et al.*, ask whether abortion protesters who conduct sit-ins and demonstrations at abortion clinics can be subjected to either the Racketeer Influenced and Corrupt Organizations Act (RICO), which was enacted to combat organized crime, or the Hobbs Act, which makes it a crime to obstruct, delay, or affect interstate commerce by robbery or extortion. "It's a great day for pro-lifers," said Troy Newman, president of Operation Rescue. Kim Gandy, president of the National Organization for Women (NOW), expressed disappointment in the ruling because the temporary injunction against protesters had decreased violence outside clinics across the nation. Scheidler's lawyer, Thomas Brejcha, called the ruling "not just a victory for pro-life activists, but for anyone who chooses to exercise his First Amendment rights to effect social change." "If protesting is extortion, then all kinds of other political protests would be extortion, and they could not be allowed under the law," lawyer Alan Untereiner said.

NOW had tried to shut down protests by using a federal law originally intended to target mobsters, claiming that the coordinated effort by antiabortionists to close down or disrupt clinics went beyond the actions of individual protesters, and should be treated much like organized crime. The NOW lawsuit alleged that protesters harassed doctors, assaulted patients and vandalized clinics.

Justice Stephen Breyer said that Congress did not create "a freestanding physical violence offense" in the Hobbs Act, but rather, Congress addressed violence at abortion clinics in 1994 when it passed the Freedom of Access to Clinic Entrances Act (FACE), which permits courts to issue injunctions to set limits for protesters. The problem with FACE, according to women's groups, is that it is a weak and ineffective instrument because it depends on the cooperation and willingness of local prosecutors to invoke it. Additionally, FACE creates inconsistent mandates on a city-by-city basis as individual judges make local rulings and set limits.

NOW has argued that by blocking access to the clinics, the protesters deprived the clinics of the use of their property and thereby violated the Hobbs Act of 1946, which prohibits the obstruction of commerce "by robbery or extortion." Gandy said the ruling "could add to the increasing difficulty women face in obtaining reproductive health services."

Antiabortion leader Joseph Scheidler predicted renewed activism at clinics but said the protests would be peaceful, adding that they "will be mostly prayer vigils and counseling. . . . The old days of Operation Rescue, I think, are pretty well finished. I don't see any reason to resurrect that—the arrests and so forth."

Abortion rights supporters are not convinced that peaceful protests will ensue. "This opinion is a green light to the people who have been orchestrating this violence behind the scenes to proceed full speed ahead," said Gandy. "What it means is that again women will be putting their bodies on the line to protect the clinics and patients."

In the following chapter, various authors argue their points in terms of providing women with abortion rights without interference and those who want to protest against those rights.

The Supreme Court Rules in Favor of Protestors

Michelle Chen

Michelle Chen is a staff writer for the NewStandard *online newspaper in Syracuse, New York.*

[O n] Tuesday [February 28, 2006], the [U.S.] Supreme Court ruled that anti-abortion violence cannot be prosecuted under federal racketeering statutes. In a ruling that stirred controversy even among progressives, the justices sealed a two-decade legal battle, striking down an effort by the nation's largest feminist group to secure harsh legal recourse against harassment and violence at women's health clinics.

Meanwhile, some activist organizations—including some typically allied with pro-choice groups—applauded the ruling as an affirmation of free speech and political expression. The ruling addressed claims brought by National Organization for Women (NOW) and two women's healthcare organizations against Joseph Scheidler, leader of the anti-abortion group Pro-Life Action Network (PLAN), and against Operation Rescue, an organization that has staged high-profile blockades of abortion clinics. The court found that the tactics of the anti-choice activists did not fall under the jurisdiction of laws aimed specifically at robbery and extortion perpetrated by criminal enterprises for financial gain.

Balancing Freedom of Speech and Intimidation

In its legal filings, NOW cited more than 120 acts of intimidation and violence perpetrated by clinic-protestors against women seeking reproductive-health services. The incidents included anti-choice activists forcibly restraining women from entering facilities, physical assaults against patients and health-care providers, and the destruction of medical equipment. . . .

Initially spurred by a spate of attacks on clinics in the 1980s, NOW has long sought legal protection for medical personnel and patients under the 1970 Racketeer Influenced and Corrupt Organizations (RICO) Act and the 1946 Hobbs Act. Primarily intended to combat organized crime, RICO established criminal sanctions against groups engaged in racketeering, and the Hobbs Act criminalized robbery, extortion and related threats that impact interstate commerce.

According to the February 28 decision, the anti-abortion protestors did not have an economic motive, which is at the crux of the racketeering statutes. Rejecting NOW's contention, the court wrote in its opinion that "physical violence unrelated to robbery or extortion falls outside the Hobbs Act's scope."

NOW denounced the Court's ruling as an affront to reproductive choice. "If women are too terrified to walk into clinics and healthcare providers are too terrified to keep their doors open," the organization said in a statement on Tuesday, "then we will have lost the fight for reproductive freedom even with *Roe v. Wade* still on the books."

Operation Rescue President Troy Newman issued a statement commending the Court for defend[ing] the liberties of anti-abortion activists.

Operation Rescue President Troy Newman issued a statement commending the Court for defend[ing] the liberties of anti-abortion activists who, Newman said, "can now exercise their First Amendment rights to speak out about abortion without fear of a RICO suit." . . .

RICO Was Not Designed to Inhibit Free Speech

Some progressive groups have sided with the anti-choice activists' stance on the issue, contending that NOW's reading of the law is dangerously broad and has turned RICO and the Hobbs Act into tools for silencing political speech.

Consistent Life, a self-described "pro-peace, pro-life" coalition of mostly religious groups involved with anti-abortion as well as anti-death penalty and anti-violence activity, led more than two-dozen activist groups in filing a friend-of-the-court brief opposing NOW's suit. The parties included secular groups, some of which do not take a public position on abortion issues. In the brief, the animal-rights organization People for the Ethical Treatment of Animals and the anti-war group Plowshares joined lesser-known organizations such as Vieques Support Committee, which has engaged in civil disobedience against United States military action on the Puerto Rican island.

In other words, there [would be] no objective protection for free speech.

The AFL-CIO and other unions have also opposed NOW's arguments, warning that if broadly interpreted, the laws could be used to suppress labor organizing.

In recent years, RICO has served corporations targeted by the radical environmental movement, enabling them to pursue legal action against activists who organize to subvert their operations. Mirroring the argument of the anti-choice groups, animal-rights activists have denounced what they see as a politically motivated overstretching of the law.

Responding to a previous Supreme Court review of the NOW case in 2002, Abraham J. Bonowitz, director of Citizens United for Alternatives to the Death Penalty issued a strong statement against NOW's position. Describing himself as "firmly and unapologetically pro-choice," he argued nonetheless that "the precedent of using RICO against protesters is far too dangerous to go unchallenged." . . .

Carol Crossed, a board member of Consistent Life, commented that under the legal framework envisioned by NOW, activists on both the Left and the Right would be "vulnerable to whatever the politics is of the particular ruling group at the time, whether they agree with us or disagree with us. In other words, there [would be] no objective protection for free speech."

Suggesting the possibility of a slippery slope, she added that had the Court agreed with NOW's interpretation of the laws, "the opponents of the rights of minorities, animal rights, environmentalism, anti-war activists [could] use this against organizations like NOW." Crossed also said that since RICO was originally intended to help law enforcement target entire criminal organizations, a case involving a political protest could encompass an organization's general membership, including those not directly connected to the action in question.

But NOW sees a clear line between non-violent political expression and politically motivated terror. The group's president, Kim Gandy, told the *NewStandard*: "The case is about a nationwide enterprise that coordinated the use of violence and threats of violence to force the closing of lawful businesses, in this case reproductive health clinics that perform abortions. There is no part of that scenario that is protected by 'free speech'—however loosely one might define that term."

Protestors Cannot Be Prosecuted

But NOW's critics on this case contend that while some protest actions may be illegal, interpreting them as extortion or racketeering distorts the law and could lead to unwarranted civil or criminal penalties against political dissent.

The Court's latest ruling contrasts with a 1994 decision holding that a racketeering claim need not provide proof of economic motives. That opinion set the stage for a 1998 trial in Chicago, in which a jury found that the systematic aggression orchestrated by Scheidler and PLAN constituted "racketeering." The case led both to monetary damages and to a nationwide injunction against anti-choice violence and harassment.

But in 2003, the Supreme Court reversed course and struck down the lower-court ruling, and Tuesday's decision addressed remaining legal questions on the scope of the Hobbs Act and private civil action under RICO with respect to anti-choice activism.

Newly appointed Justice Samuel Alito did not participate in the decision on the case, which the Court heard last term.

Other forms of legal recourse are still available to victims of abortion-clinic violence. The 1994 Freedom of Access to Clinic Entrances (FACE) Act, which NOW helped craft, bars the use of intimidation or physical force to block entrance to reproductive healthcare facilities.

But Gandy noted that the FACE Act targets the perpetrators of the violence, not the organizations or leaders behind it. Referring to the arson and bombing incidents that have illustrated the extremes of the anti-choice movement in the past, she said that RICO "lets you get to the 'kingpin' of an operation . . . who never themselves lit a match or pulled a trigger, but directed the actions of others."

Killing Abortion Providers Is Justifiable Homicide

Chuck Spingola

Chuck Spingola is a minister who travels around the United States crusading against abortion.

I recently read an article about Clay Waagner entitled, "The Quiet Fall of an American terrorist" [December 10, 2003]. The article, written by Frederick Clarkson, rightly identified Clay Waagner, Eric Rudolph and James Kopp as Christian terrorists. [Eleanor] Ellie Smeal, President of the Feminist Majority Foundation notes, "But the investigative work that would lead you to the next one (Christian terrorist) is falling short. There are people still at large who aided and abetted Kopp and Rudolph. . . . The odds are we are not done with this, and we won't be until the core that has been encouraging violence, itself unravels." Comparing the statistical death tally of 44,000,000 innocent babies compared to 7 guilty abortionists you would think Mrs. Smeal would apply her statements to those who murdered the former group rather than the latter, but not so. Does Mrs. Smeal mean to put in jail all those who believe in and or acted upon the defensive action doctrine? This brings the prediction of the conspiracy theorists one step closer to reality.

The Christian War on Abortion

The federal Department of Justice's "war on terrorism" will not only be waged against the Muslim nations but also Christian terrorists in our homeland. One might ask what do the Muslims and Christians have in common? The Holy Bible and Koran both condemn baby murder and homosexuality as capital crimes. The radical elements of both religions are willing

Chuck Spingola, "Thanks Be to God and the Christian Terrorist," www.armyofgod.com, January 5, 2004. Reproduced by permission.

to do more than talk to resist the societal promotion of both these capital crimes. The foreign terrorists (Muslim) resist the imposition of the United States/United Nations charter, which promotes "population control" (abortion) and "diversity" (homosexuality), while the Christian/domestic terrorist simply resists the "law" of the land, which promotes and often subsidizes abortion and homosexuality.

The article noted, "There was a time in 2001 when for the first time in history, three of the FBI's [Federal Bureau of Investigation] ten most wanted criminals were antiabortion domestic terrorists." What a sad commentary this is! The days of womb children murderers being found on the FBI's ten most wanted list is over. We have devolved. Now, in 2001, 30% of the Feds ten most wanted are notoriously listed as criminals for defending womb children from their paid assassins. Magistrates and their government agencies must be "able men, such as fear God, men of truth, hating covetousness" (Exod. 18:21). Civil and military leaders who meet these qualifications have been, for the most part, purged from positions of leadership in the United States of America at an accelerated rate over the past 15 years. Judge Roy Moore is a prime example of this. [Moore was removed as chief justice of the Supreme Court of Alabama because of his refusal to remove a monument of the Ten Commandments from the Courthouse when ordered to do so by a federal court.]

I often weep over the oppression and persecution of the Christian terrorist in this country.

Christian Terrorists Are Righteous

"For rulers are not a terror to good works, but to the evil. Wilt thou then not be afraid of the power? Do that which is good, and thou shalt have praise of the same: For he is the minister of God to thee for good. But if thou do that which is evil, be afraid; for he beareth not the sword in vain: for he is the minister of God, a revenger to execute wrath upon him that doeth evil." Rom. 13:3–4

Considering what Romans chapter 13 has to say about rulers, it could logically be concluded that the Christian terrorists Waagner, Rudolph, Kopp, etc., qualify as "minister(s) of God" more so than America's Department of "Justice" and its subsequent agencies. Indeed, the wicked should be terrified of good men. Impenitent baby murderers, sodomites, adulterers, man stealers, pedophiles, rapists, etc., should indeed cringe in the shadows at the presence of a God fearing man even as they would cringe before Jesus because they are to act as his body on earth, receiving Him as their Governor. I have heard it said that Christian terrorist Clay Waagner did some things wrong before and during his 10-month reign of terror. It has been said that he does not deserve hero status or recognition because he is a bank robber and car thief. Perhaps it should also be noted that this bank robbing, car thieving terrorist is directly responsible for saving the lives of 5,000 innocent babies. His reward will most likely be life without the possibility of parole. Waagner's response is, "A small price to pay." So what have brother Clay Waagner detractors done so great as to qualify them to stand in judgment of his deeds? Prudence would suggest we leave his war time actions for God to judge, and give honor to whom honor is due. Chalk up another Halleluia and a hip hip hooray for the Christian who terrorized the entire nation's abortion industry without firing a shot. . . .

The salt has lost its savor. For the most part the wicked are no longer terrified of the God fearing man. Where there is no fear of God's people, there is no fear of God.

"How is the faithful city become an harlot! it was full of judgment; righteousness lodged in it; but now murderers." Isa. 1:21

Support for the Christian Terrorist

The wicked civilian and the Federal Government appear to be coconspirators in their coup to overthrow Christ and his people. Queer Boy Scoutmasters, abortion on demand, and same sex marriage is all part and parcel of this godless takeover of God's America.

Pleading, politics, and pandering have done precious little to stop the holocaust against the innocent.

Those blessed few that actually do terrify the wicked are vigorously denounced and punished by the government "of the people." I often weep over the oppression and persecution of the Christian terrorist in this country for it accomplishes three goals. First, it comforts and strengthens the wicked. Second, it discourages the would-be CT [Christian terrorist] from action. Third, it makes the CT feel alone in his cause.

Most of the time when I leave the killing place, my self-esteem diminishes as I have failed where others have succeeded. The baby butchers and their subordinates were not terrified at my presence nor from my actions. I think to myself, "I did not save the life of one person slated for death." Today, 4,400 babies were murdered yet again, because yesterday the killers would not be TALKED out of their crimes. Pleading, politics, and pandering have done precious little to stop the holocaust against the innocent, their death toll rising to 44,000,000 in the last 30 years. Oh, but the Christian terrorist is not so inadequate. Dead abortionists don't kill babies, and a fire bombed death camp can no longer facilitate the holocaust against them.

As cream rising to the top of the milk, so the Christian terrorist rises above the huddled masses of churchgoers and the many voices which denounce their violent attempts to defend the innocent from their murderous assailants. Regarding abortion, the separation is clear. The CT has the Word of God and a testimony of loving, albeit terrifying (to the wicked), actions. And when he had opened the fifth seal, I saw under the altar the souls of them that were slain for the word of God, and for the testimony which they held. (Rev. 6:9)

Never before in the history of the United States has there been reason for a God fearing man to be vexed to the core of his being such as now.

The huddled masses of churchgoers have the Word of God alone, interpreted through fear colored glasses and played upon tinkling symbols and sounding brass. "Be ye warmed and filled" they sing to the womb child slated for death. Adding insult to injury, they not only discriminate against the pre-born but also denounce those who will not do likewise. This was no more apparent than on September 3, 2003 [the day Paul Hill, a former minister, was executed for the 1994 murder of Dr. John Britton, who performed abortions]. The day's events "outed" many a "Christian/pro-life" Clergyman. Indeed this could have been their best opportunity to secure "the uppermost rooms at feasts, and the chief seats in the synagogues." Like media savvy Pharisees voicing government sanctioned opinions, so were they in their denunciation of Hill's actions.

On this day, without the benefit of a trial, the Reverend Paul Jennings Hill was to receive his reward for shooting a known mass murderer of babies, death in Florida's execution chamber.

And they cried with a loud voice, saying, How long, O Lord, holy and true, dost thou not judge and avenge our blood on them that dwell on the earth? And white robes were given unto every one of them; and it was said unto them, that they should rest yet for a little season, until their fellowservants also and their brethren, that should be killed as they were, should be fulfilled. (Rev. 6:10–11.)

Fighting for the Unborn

Never before in the history of the United States has there been reason for a God fearing man to be vexed to the core of his being such as now. There is no end in sight to baby murder. Pleading, politics, and pandering have done precious little to stop the holocaust against the innocent. Four thousand more will be murdered today. Turning your back on them is to turn your back on Christ, leaving you robbed of your manhood and soul's salvation. Defending the babies with force unleashes all the powers of the United States Department of Justice upon your head. On the FBI's 10 most wanted list you will be hounded and persecuted by many and to no end.

Let's consider other options. There must be something that can be done to save a baby that is pleasing to God and the government at the same time. Yes, it is possible to save a baby, one here and one there, as the heroic sidewalk counselor does. Even the attempt diminishes the culpability of inaction; does it not? Saving babies within the government sanctioned methods is better than nothing, right? As we consider these questions let us praise God Almighty for the brave Christian that flat out terrorizes the wicked. Like the terrified masses praying for death rather than face the wrath of the Lamb, let us pray that all the politicians, judges, and those who otherwise assisted the baby butchers will be terrified to death before tomorrow's baby killing begins. Shall we?

> And the kings of the earth, and the great men, and the rich men, and the chief captains, and the mighty men, and every bondman, and every free man, hid themselves in the dens and in the rocks of the mountains; And said to the mountains and rocks, Fall on us, and hide us from the face of him that sitteth on the throne, and from the wrath of the Lamb; for the great day of his wrath is come; and who shall be able to stand? (Rev. 6:15–17).

Protesters Harass Patients and Invade Their Privacy

Center for Reproductive Rights

The Center for Reproductive Rights is a nonprofit legal advocacy organization dedicated to promoting and defending women's reproductive rights worldwide.

Although federal and state FACE [Freedom of Access to Clinic Entrances Act] laws have successfully crushed some of the most extreme violence and physical blockades at clinics, they do not adequately protect against the many forms of harassment that clinics suffer from on a regular basis. Every year, a majority of clinics experience at least one of five types of harassment: picketing; picketing coupled with physical contact or blocking patients or staff; vandalism; picketing of staff members' homes; and bomb threats. Eighty-two percent of large reproductive health care facilities, which perform 94% of all abortions in the United States, experience one or more types of harassment in a given year.

Disruptive picketing (defined as protest activity that harasses, intimidates, and impedes the movement of staff or patients) is an increasingly common means of harassing clinic patients and staff. In 2002, clinics reported over 10,000 incidents of disruptive picketing, and a majority of clinics experience picketing at least 20 times a year. Clinics have also recently reported the rise of webcam use among protesters, who have posted pictures of patients and staff, as well as listed their names and license plate numbers, on anti-choice websites. Advocates and providers expect this disturbing trend in privacy invasion to continue to develop.

Center for Reproductive Rights, "Picketing and Harassment," www.reproductiverights .org, February 19, 2007. © 2003 The Center. All rights reserved. Reproduced by permission.

The Health of Patients Is at Risk

Not only does intimidating protest activity cause tremendous psychological stress to clinic staff and patients, but it may also adversely affect patients' physical health. Patients who face confrontational protesters may experience raised blood pressure levels, which may weaken their health and complicate the procedures they undergo. The threatening appearance of protest activity has deterred patients from entering clinic facilities, even when they require immediate medical attention or when delaying the performance of a scheduled procedure increased the risk posed to the patient.

Unless the disruptive picketing escalates to a level of violence that constitutes a violation of the federal FACE law or a state equivalent, other legal remedies must be sought to assist abortion providers, clinic staff and patients who experience harassment and intimidation. Pro-choice advocates have attempted to hold anti-abortion activists responsible for their disruptions to clinics' daily functioning and provision of services by suing them for criminal racketeering and extortion. Advocates have also attempted to prosecute protesters under state criminal laws (such as trespass or loitering). The most successful means of redressing disruptive picketing, however, has been the establishment of protective zones around clinics by states and municipalities.

Creating Protection Zones

To protect abortion providers and patients from intimidation and harassment by anti-abortion protesters, cities and states have passed legislation creating no-protest zones around entrances to reproductive health care facilities. By carving out protest-free space around clinic entrances, such legislation enables patients and clinic staff to freely enter and exit clinics without being bombarded with anti-abortion materials and intimidated by confrontational "in your face" protesters. Such zones have also been established via court injunction.

Floating Protective Zones ("bubbles"): One way that legislatures have promoted safe access to clinics is by passing legislation that creates floating protective zones (or floating "bubble" zones). Floating protective zone legislation requires protesters within a stated proximity to reproductive health care facilities to maintain a certain distance from patients and staff. These zones of privacy, which "float" around pedestrians as they enter and exit clinics, establish a zone of separation between protesters and patients.

For example, a Colorado law prohibits protesters from approaching within 8 feet of a patient or staff member within 100 feet of any health care facility unless the person consents to being approached. The Supreme Court affirmed the constitutionality of this law in its 2000 decision, *Hill v. Colorado*, a case brought by anti-abortion protesters challenging the floating protective zones as an impingement on their First Amendment rights. Paving the way for more floating protective zone legislation in the future, the Court concluded that the law legitimately restricted demonstration activity because it advanced the state's important interests in protecting women's access to abortion services and in promoting public health and safety.

The following year, the Massachusetts legislature passed a similar law establishing 6-foot floating protective zones around all pedestrians within 15 feet of a reproductive health care facility. The First Circuit recently affirmed the constitutionality of this speech restriction as well.

Fixed Protective Zones ("buffers"): The state may also protect safe access to abortion clinics by establishing fixed protective zones (or "buffer" zones) around reproductive health care facilities. Fixed protective zones are areas of specified length and width around entrances to reproductive health care facilities within which protesters are prohibited from engaging in certain activity. Many of these fixed protective zones were created under injunctions issued by state and federal courts in order to protect clinics that have experienced disruptive picketing and harassment. The Supreme Court has twice affirmed the constitutionality of these speech restrictions. In addition, several municipalities, such as Los Angeles, Denver and St. Paul have enacted local ordinances that establish fixed protective zones around all local clinics. These speech regulations have also withstood legal challenges from protesters claiming violations of their First Amendment rights.

Other Protective Legislation: In addition to creating protective zones around patients/staff and around clinic entrances, legislatures are also attempting to address protester behavior in other ways. For example, in the 2003 legislative session, the Massachusetts legislature introduced a bill banning photography taken around clinic entrances with the intent of invading a patient's privacy, coercing her out of reproductive health services, or threatening her with bodily harm. This bill seeks to curb a growing trend among anti-abortion protesters of photographing patients and staff entering and exiting clinics and posting their images on websites.

Abortion Providers Should Not Have to Work with Fear, Threats, and Violence

Sarah Todd

Sarah Todd is an assistant professor at Carleton University in Ottawa, Ontario, Canada, and the author of numerous articles.

Whether [the anthrax threat] is a hoax or not, it's a criminal act and that act will be prosecuted to the fullest extent of the law. . . . It hit innocent people and I want to make sure that we do everything we can to protect those public servants.

> The people buying gas masks are trying to impose a shred of control over a potential threat that is silent, invisible. A monster that could arrive in the morning mail, on an autumn breeze, in your next breath. At least that's the fear.

Recently, I have found myself reading half-a-dozen breathless and fearful articles . . . describing the risk that anthrax poses for government and media employees. This threat has, at least momentarily, become a credible issue for workers. As someone who has worked in an abortion clinic, watching my mail for "powdery substances" is not an unusual practice. It has been a year since I was an abortion counsellor at a clinic in a large Canadian hospital. I remember the anthrax information session and the blue binder filled with protocols to be followed if clinic staff were exposed to this "dangerous powder." I remember opening unfamiliar packages with caution. What strikes me about recent news reports is how anthrax is perceived as a "new" danger for Americans and, to a lesser extent Canadians. This "new" threat, while no less deliberate and

Sarah Todd, "Secrecy and Safety: Health Care Workers in Abortion Clinics," *Notebook/ Carnet, Labour/Le Travail*, issue 52, fall 2003. Copyright © 2003 The Canadian Committee on Labour History. Reproduced by permission.

focussed than the anthrax risks to which abortion service providers are accustomed, is perceived as a broad social concern, whereas our earlier fears are not considered to be a general threat. Instead, the safety concerns of abortion workers are contained within abortion debates. . . .

Health Care, Politics and Safety

Three assertions ground my discussion. First, since 1988, abortions have been recognized as a legal health care service. As such, this exploration of the conditions under which abortion workers practice will focus on our experience as "everyday" practitioners of health care. In fact, abortion workers' daily tasks (and thus working experience) differ little from the employment experiences of any health care provider. Our days are full of providing accessible, safe, supportive, and responsible health care to people who have a right to these services. We are housekeeping staff, social workers, physicians, nurses, receptionists, and technicians. In these roles we provide, for the most part, ordinary health care services and go home to ordinary lives.

Though most anti-abortion violence has been aimed at physicians . . . [various] staff have all been terrorized, wounded, or killed because of their work in abortion clinics.

Second, workers in abortion clinics are often not pro-choice activists or "radicals." Although most workers in these settings are committed to women's access to legal and safe abortions, the cultural and religious ambivalence that surrounds abortion is also reflected in our daily struggles with the nature of our jobs. In addition, when clinics operate within a hospital setting, some of the health care professionals engaged in this work have little choice as to whether or not their technical skills are implicated in the provision of abortion services. As a result, many health care professionals approach their work in abortion clinics, not as a political practice, but as part of an imagined politically-neutral health care system.

Finally, the daily practices of abortion workers take place within a hostile, often dangerous environment. Anthrax threats—sending powdered substances to clinics with notes inferring that the contents are anthrax—appeared as a method of harassing abortion clinic staff in the late 1990s. This was, however, just the most recent manifestation of what have been several decades of violence. For some time, many of us working in Canadian abortion clinics could rationalize that, however tragic, these types of dangers only existed for clinics in the United States. Then, on 24 January 1992, Dr. [Henry] Morgentaler's clinic in Toronto was bombed; on 8 November 1994, Dr. [Garson] Romalis was shot and wounded in his Vancouver home; and on 11 November 1995, Dr. [Hugh] Short, a Hamilton doctor, was also shot and wounded while in his home. In 1996, there was a butyric acid attack on the Morgentaler Clinic in Alberta, and in 1997, Dr. [Jack] Fainman was shot and injured at his home in Winnipeg. Though most anti-abortion violence has been aimed at physicians, clinic receptionists, nurses, and security staff have all been terrorized, wounded, or killed because of their work in abortion clinics.

Each day I returned home from work to see the sign sitting there, unsure as to whether I needed to be concerned for my safety.

This type of sustained yet unpredictable violence is, as Dr. Morgentaler has suggested, "a terror tactic to spread panic among people who are providing abortion services." On this level, it is an effective strategy. A number of studies suggest that anti-abortion violence results in fear and stress among clinic staff. These events form the basis for my third assertion, that abortion workers are employed in a context that is perceived by them (there is sufficient evidence to suggest that this perception is grounded in reality) to involve a significant degree of personal risk. This risk takes two forms: the fear and actual experience of physical harm and a pervading social stigmatization. Each has a particular effect on workers, shaping their sense of workplace safety or lack thereof. . . .

Workers Deal with Fear, Isolation, and Social Stigma

The silence that surrounds abortion work magnifies workers' insecurities and increases the isolation many of us feel in our jobs. It is not only the fear of physical violence that constitutes the hostile environment in which we work. It is also our fear of social stigma that regulates silence regarding abortion and subsequently leaves us dealing with our safety concerns alone. The pervasiveness of this stigma was never more evident to me than when the very women to whom we provided services expressed that they could not understand how we could be involved in this work; even some of the women who access abortion services consider it to be dirty work. Many abortion workers find it difficult, if not impossible, to tell friends, neighbours, and often even family members about our jobs. Our vulnerability, and thus our constant heightened awareness that friends and neighbours might discover "what we do," is often a source of ongoing stress. To illustrate, shortly after clinic staff received a fax confirming that pro-life groups had all of our names and addresses, my neighbours posted a sign in their front window with the slogan "justice for the unborn." I was completely unnerved, uncertain as to whether this was a statement for the general public or a message aimed directly at me. Each day I returned home from work to see the sign sitting there, unsure as to whether I needed to be concerned for my safety. It is these broader workplace hazards that make abortion workers' concerns even more difficult to contain within mainstream notions of worker safety. When the danger that originates in our workplaces slips incessantly into our private spheres, our ability to find ways to address these concerns within existing frameworks seems grossly inadequate. At the same time, perhaps the problems that abortion work presents provide an opportunity to consider the multiple ways in which many aspects of workers' safety fail to be contained within spaces of employment.

We had internalized the notion that violence, intimidation, and fear were 'just part of the job.'

Another challenge in addressing the safety concerns of abortion workers is that the dangers faced by health care workers more generally have only been brought to light in the past decade or so. Abortion workers' experience of verbal harassment, placard-carrying protesters, hospital staff placing various religious paraphernalia in the clinic, and staff silences and avoidances all serve to imbue our workplace with a virtual miasma of threat and uncertainty. . . . The police have, at times, recommended that we vary our routes home. In this atmosphere of vague threats, perpetual caution, and little institutional or social support, our emotional responses are often difficult to organize in terms of paranoia versus legitimate caution, which also makes it difficult to discuss our work fears. Why should a pro-life bumper sticker on a car in the hospital parking lot raise my anxiety as I ride up the elevator? Then again, why should it not? This lack of a space in which we can confidently assess our fears as legitimate or otherwise ensures the silences regarding our work continue. We are left vulnerable and isolated. . . .

Funding Affects Safety

What might be possible to consider within existing frameworks for debating worker safety is the broad restructuring of the health care system and the institutional structure in which many Canadian abortion clinics operate. The relationship between clinics and their parent hospitals has always been ambivalent. In 1995, Carole Joffe noted that even after the legalization of abortion services there was a significant degree of institutional resistance against their provision. In today's neoliberal economy, this relationship has the potential to become even more strained. For instance, hospitals increasingly rely on private donations as opposed to government funding; abortion services threaten those types of donations. If hospitals are forced to prioritize the acquisition of private funding, what will happen to the place of abortion services within the hospital system and what will these changes mean for patients and staff? Fiscal concerns have also resulted in an increase in part-time labour and the out sourcing of services such as security, which presents new challenges to clinic staff who are often forced to depend upon less specialized security personnel who may know little about the specific safety concerns of abortion work. Shifts to the private sector often ignore the special needs of hospitals, particularly abortion clinics.

Our responses signify the cultural ambivalence we have toward health care workers who provide abortion services.

The dynamics that evolve from these new funding relations result in a less supportive workplace, and increase the need to keep one's work secret from other hospital staff. This atmosphere is further complicated as our roles change. We find that our jobs are becoming more rationalized and routinized, with an increased emphasis on technical aspects and less of a focus on caring and interpersonal relations. Although many of us draw on the caring components of our practice to deflect our attention away from our fears and ambivalences, organizational pressures mean that "caring" has little significance in our overall work performance. These changes in health care are seldom considered in terms of their possible impact on abortion work, particularly in its location as dirty work. When workplace discussions increasingly focus on technicalities, our safety concerns seldom receive formal responses from hospital administrators or proactive preventative work from unions. Instead, safety issues are left largely in the hands of clinic staff. I think we seldom ever asked administration or union staff to become involved in our concerns because we had internalized the notion that violence, intimidation, and fear were "just part of the job". . . .

All Workers Deserve a Safe Environment

The changes in health care priorities will have a particular impact on the safety concerns of abortion workers. What will it mean to have part-time workers rotating through clinics? Will this type of employment structure not diminish the informal structures that offer staff security and safety? The caring component of our work is one of the few aspects that help workers negotiate its rather slippery moral terrain: if that falls away, what will be left? These are all significant aspects of considering worker safety. They are also the issues that concern all health care workers. How will health care restructuring affect our understandings of worker safety?

The ways in which our society responded to the anthrax concerns of postal workers as a general threat to Canadian workers is interesting when compared to our earlier responses to similar fears expressed by abortion workers. Our responses signify the cultural ambivalence we have toward health care workers who provide abortion services. This is to the detriment of all workers, but particularly the nurses, social workers, ultrasound technicians, receptionists, security staff, housekeeping staff, and physicians who are struggling through the day-to-day safety issues involved in abortion work. Unless we begin to find ways to explore abortion work from the perspective of workplace safety, the important issues that are facing these workers will continue to be ignored. Abortion work is principally a regular health care service carried out, for the most part, by unsupported health care providers in an extraordinarily hostile environment. At a time of enormous transition within the health care system, and in our current heightened sense of insecurity, it is important that the uneasiness of these workers be recognized as credible concerns for workers in general.

CHAPTER 5

Should Aborted Fetuses Be Used for Medical Research?

Chapter Preface

Recent studies suggest that embryonic stem cells may hold the secret to treatment or cures for some of the most debilitating diseases, including Alzheimer's and Parkinson's. In political terms, however, the research has been stalled. Opponents believe that an embryo is life, and destruction of these embryos is tantamount to murder, even if the embryos are destined to be discarded, often as a result of excess embryos stored at in vitro fertilization clinics. Another option is for scientists to use stem cells from aborted fetuses. This procedure is most vehemently opposed by pro-life activists who do not support stem cell research. Opponents argue that adult stem cells provide the same results, thereby making fetal stem cell research unnecessary. But scientists argue that adult stem cells do not show the same promise as fetal stem cells since the adult cells are pretty much fixed and do not appear to grow or replicate themselves as readily or successfully as fetal stem cells.

In August 2001 President George W. Bush limited federal funding for stem cell research to just 60 stem cell lines that had previously been developed. But scientists argue that fewer than 22 lines were actually available because of a variety of factors, including contamination. Recent polls indicate that 70 percent of Americans support fetal stem cell research, and many politicians do as well. Senator Orrin Hatch (R-Utah) said, "I do not question that an embryo is a living cell. But I do not believe that a frozen embryo in a fertility clinic freezer constitutes human life."

Yet, other politicians disagree. Senator David Vitter (R-Louisiana) said he firmly believes that neither "Congress, independent researchers nor any human being should be allowed, in effect, to play God by determining that one life is more valuable than another." Senator Sam Brownback (R-Kansas) has stated that "The government should not be in the business of funding this ethically troubling research with taxpayer dollars," adding that using embryos for such research amounts to "treating humans as raw material."

Religious leaders, too, adamantly oppose fetal stem cell use. Father Tadeusz Pacholczyk, director of the National Catholic Bioethics Center in Philadelphia, Pennsylvania, stated that, "Young humans have now been reduced to biomedical waste ... and I truly believe that the true measure of greatness of a society is always measured by how it treats its weakest members."

Michael Tanner, director of health and welfare studies at the Cato Institute (a nonprofit public policy research foundation), maintains that the debate is really about using government money to fund the research. When the Family Research Council issued a press release that emphasized the failures of embryonic stem cell research, Tanner stated that their agenda is "ultimately a moral position, but they insist on portraying it as a scientific one." Both sides of the debate end up distorting the scientific facts in order to further their own agendas, he asserts. He contends that supporters believe the research is a means to cure diseases and save lives, and opponents do not want to have their tax dollars to pay for something they believe is morally offensive.

President Bush has doubts about the effectiveness of fetal stem cell research and has restricted using federal funds in this endeavor. He has stated that "scientists believed fetal tissue research offered great hope for cures and treatments, yet the progress to date has not lived up to its initial expectations." President Bush believes that there are alternative research methods, such as research on umbilical cords, placenta, and adult stem cells, which do not create any moral dilemmas.

The authors in the following chapter argue the merits of fetal stem cell research, discuss the moral dilemmas, and offer alternatives that may deem fetal stem cell research obsolete.

Stem Cell Research Plays a Critical Role in Medicine

Julie Hutto

Julie Hutto is a research assistant for the Technology & News Economy Project at the Progressive Policy Institute in Washington, D.C.

In the wake of a stunning rebuke of his stem cell policy by moderate Republicans in the House of Representatives, President [George W.] Bush is promising to use the first veto of his administration on the Stem Cell Research Enhancement Act of 2005. The bill, passed in the House on May 24 [2005,] with a bipartisan majority of 238 votes—including 50 Republicans—would allow federal funding to be used for medical research on new lines of stem cells derived from human embryos when the parents of those embryos have signed statements saying they will otherwise be destroyed. The legislation now awaits action in the Senate. The Progressive Policy Institute urges the Senate leadership to allow a vote on it, and hopes a large majority of senators will support it, even in the face of a veto threat. [The Senate approved the bill on July 18, 2006. President Bush vetoed it the next day.]

It is time to admit that the president's four-year-old stem cell policy experiment has failed, and the damage must be undone. In the summer of 2001, Bush decided to limit federal funding for potentially life-saving medical research on embryonic stem cells to a few existing lines of cells. Today, the results of that policy are painfully clear: Federally funded research on the approved lines remains anemic, because the lines have proven to be inadequate for robust studies. Meanwhile, medical researchers in other countries are regularly making international headlines with new breakthroughs.

Julie Hutto, "Embryonic Stem Cell Research: A Renewed Call for Robust Federal Support," *Front and Center*, June 2, 2005. Reproduced by permission.

Religious Beliefs Stand in the Way of Research

The administration and most Republicans in Congress are standing against the opinion of a solid majority of Americans, including many in their own party. A May 2005 CBS News survey found that 58 percent of Americans approve of medical research on embryonic stem cells. Another May 2005 survey by CNN/Gallup/USA found that 53 percent specifically support easing the current restrictions on federal funding. Furthermore, Mike Castle (R-Del.) joined Diana DeGette (D-Colo.) in sponsoring the Stem Cell Research Enhancement Act—and a number of anti-abortion Republican legislators, including Sens. Orrin Hatch (R-Utah) and Trent Lott (R-Miss.), and Reps. Joe Barton (R-Texas) and Jo Ann Emerson (R-Mo.), also support the bill.

Other opponents of embryonic stem cell research lean on dubious science in their reasoning.

Why are the president and his remaining Republican allies in Congress so adamant in their opposition to embryonic stem cell research? The simple answer is that they are trying to mollify activists in the religious right who believe that human life is sacrosanct from the moment cells begin joining together, or even earlier. House Majority Leader Tom DeLay (R-Tex.) explicitly made that connection when he called the passage of the Stem Cell Research Enhancement Act a "vote to fund with taxpayer dollars the dismemberment of living, distinct human beings for the purposes of medical experimentation." Yet one of the most glaring hypocrisies in the stem cell debate relates to in vitro fertilization (IVF), which provides the embryos used for stem cell research. Intellectual consistency would suggest that legislators who support the current ban—such as Rep. Henry Hyde (R-Ill.), who has called on Congress to respect "the humanity of every fetus"—also ban IVF.

Other opponents of embryonic stem cell research lean on dubious science in their reasoning. For example, some argue—incorrectly—that there are equally promising alternatives to embryonic stem cells available to researchers. Sen. Rick Santorum (R-Pa.) recently claimed that "adult and other post-natal stem cells have been successful alternatives to embryonic stem cells and are extracted from such non-controversial sources . . . as placentas, fat, cadaver brains, bone marrow, and tissues of the spleen, pancreas, and other organs." In fact, while adult and umbilical cord stem cells can help with a small number of disorders, they lack the regenerative flexibility of embryonic stem cells to potentially treat a wide array of medical conditions. They are also more likely to contain DNA abnormalities.

If not used for medical research, the vast majority of these unused embryos would be frozen for indefinite periods, or destroyed.

The Stem Cell Research Enhancement Act is actually modest in its scope. It would simply overturn the president's ban, expanding federally funded stem cell research to stem cell lines created after his arbitrary cut-off date of August 9, 2001. The currently allowable lines are grossly inadequate to support research, so the ban has drastically slowed the advance of breakthrough medical treatments that could potentially alleviate or even cure chronic and lethal conditions that afflict nearly 130 million Americans. The legislation also contains key provisions to reaffirm oversight by the National Institutes of Health (NIH), mandate embryo donor consent, and prohibit payment for donations. It does not, however, open federal money for actually creating new stem cell lines from human embryos. That has been prohibited since the early 1990s when Congress first passed the so-called Dickey amendment, an annual rider to the Health and Human Services appropriations bill that bans the use of federal money for any research that harms human embryos, or knowingly subjects them to risks greater than those allowed on fetuses in utero.

How Stem Cell Science Works

Embryonic stem cells come from days-old human embryos, called blastocysts—hollow, microscopic balls of about 150 cells. Scientists usually obtain these embryos from fertility clinics, which create more than their patients can use in order to increase the chances of successful pregnancies through IVF. If not used for medical research, the vast majority of these unused embryos would be frozen for indefinite periods, or destroyed.

To create a new stem cell line, scientists perform the process of derivation on the embryo. Since this process destroys the embryo, it is often the most controversial element of the research.

Some embryonic stem cells, called pluripotent stem cells, can develop into any kind of cells (such as skin, nerve, or heart cells), which could be used as replacement cells for patients suffering from medical conditions such as Parkinson's disease, strokes, diabetes, multiple sclerosis, or blood, bone, and marrow disorders. Stem cell research could also lead to the development of replacement organs, supplying a much-needed resource in the face of organ donation shortages.

Ban Limits Funding

The basic case for federally funded research on embryonic stem cells is the same today as it was in 2001, when PPI [Progressive Policy Institute] released a detailed report on the issue. But developments in the past four years have further underscored the need for it. For instance, under current policy, only 21 stem cell lines are eligible for federally funded research, a fraction of the 60 to 80 lines President Bush said would be available when he announced his policy. But hundreds of lines are needed for genetically diverse research. Worse yet, since President Bush's 2001 declaration, scientists have determined that they cannot use any of the allowable lines in clinical trials or to find cures to human diseases, because the lines are contaminated with mouse feeder cells. This is because in the past scientists included layers of mouse cells, also known as feeder layers, in the petri dishes where they grew stem cell lines. These cells, however, can contain viruses and toxic proteins. A human patient's immune system would reject an organ created from contaminated stem cells if it had antibodies from these latent viruses. Some newer, privately derived stem cell lines are free of mouse cell contamination but scientists cannot use federal funds to study these.

Some private donors have also tried to fill the federal funding deficit, and such funding has led to several breakthroughs in the past few years.

Several states, most recently Connecticut and Massachusetts, have responded to the federal funding deficit with their own legislation and funds for stem cell research. In a November 2004 referendum, California pledged $3 billion for stem cell research over the next decade. Acting New Jersey Gov. Richard Codey also announced robust funding for stem cell research ($380 million), but budget shortfalls have held up the funds. In addition, Illinois, Maryland, New York, Texas, and Wisconsin are all considering legislation that either pledges funding for stem cell research or expresses support for the research. Meanwhile, legislation under consideration in Hawaii and North Carolina would fund studies into whether or not to support stem cell research there.

Some private donors have also tried to fill the federal funding deficit, and such funding has led to several breakthroughs in the past few years. The Harvard Stem Cell Institute, for instance, derived 17 new embryonic stem cell lines in

March 2004. Later that year, a Chicago fertility clinic produced 12 additional lines. However, private funding for stem cell research is limited because it is still in the most basic stages, and pharmaceutical companies view the research as too risky and the benefits too far off.

While state and private funding for stem cell research provide tangible evidence of Americans' support for the research, the patchwork of private and state-funded efforts is a second-rate solution to the federal funding gap for several reasons. First, to limit federally funded research but allow unfettered private and state-funded research slows the search for cures but does not prevent the destruction of embryos. A partial ban also falls disproportionately on academic scientists, who rely heavily on NIH grants for their research. Second, federally funded stem cell research falls under the auspices of NIH ethical guidelines, so it is subject to the most transparent, public, and rigorous oversight. NIH requires that scientists only use federal funds for research on stem cell lines derived from embryos donated for IVF, a guideline that is reiterated in the new House bill, but that policy may not hold in a state-by-state system. Moreover, proposals funded under these guidelines are publicly accountable and represent the best possible consensus on this research because they have been thoroughly vetted and submitted for public comment. Additionally, because federally funded stem cell research follows NIH guidelines, expanding it helps to ensure that the United States can take the lead in shaping international research ethics.

The U.S. Will Lose Its Research Leadership

The dogged inflexibility of the president and his Republican allies also threatens America's global leadership on medical research and biotechnology. As they have dug in their heels, several other countries, notably Great Britain and South Korea, have greatly increased governmental funding for stem cell research in the past few years. The British government not only funds research on stem cell lines derived through private funds, it directly funds the derivation of new lines. One of the latest British initiatives was a $30 million commitment to stem cell research at Cambridge University. Similarly, unlike in the United States, stem cell research in South Korea has the explicit backing of the president and has received $27 million in funding from the South Korean government since 2002. South Korean scientists have since leapt forward by cloning human embryos, extracting embryonic stem cells from them, and showing that these cells can be made to grow into different body tissues, a process known as therapeutic cloning. (That process may eventually lead to organ transplants in which the organs are grown from the patients' own cells, which could avoid the grave risk of patients rejecting donated organs.) In May 2005, the same research team, financed by the South Korean government, trumpeted their own breakthrough when they discovered a more efficient method to derive stem cell lines. Using this method, they successfully created stem cell lines that were genetic matches for nine patients of varying ages. While Bush's 2001 edict has not yet been followed by a major exodus of top stem cell researchers out of the United States, in the future more may choose, as noted scientist Roger Pederson already has, to move to countries that are aggressively pursuing stem cell research.

Scientists around the world are increasingly excited about the prospects that stem cell research could yield new treatments and cures for myriad chronic diseases. Progressives in the United States should support them in their research efforts. Thoughtfully regulated federal funding under the auspices of NIH guidelines—as the Stem Cell Research Enhancement Act proposes—would be the best way to ensure that stem cell research fulfills its potential.

Therapeutic Cloning Is Not a Form of Abortion

Dena S. Davis

Dena S. Davis is an author and a professor at Cleveland-Marshall College of Law at Cleveland State University, where she teaches a variety of courses in bioethics.

The current controversy over federal funding for research involving stem cells derived from very early embryos is situated between two other equally difficult issues: abortion and cloning. As Laurie Zoloth (2002) says, talk about stem cells is "directly proximate" to the abortion debate. Nonetheless, a settled position in favor of abortion rights does not necessarily lead to support for research that involves the death of embryos. Nor should opposition to reproductive cloning necessarily entail opposition to therapeutic cloning. There are important ways in which our attitudes toward research with embryotic stem cells ought to be entwined with our thinking about abortion and cloning, but there are also some very important distinctions which are getting lost in the noisy debate.

Stem Cell Research Is Not Abortion

> *Thinking clearly and well about stem cell research requires us to give up slogans and knee-jerk reactions.*

With regard to abortion, it is important to remember that the embryos from which stem cells are derived have never been and will never be within a woman's body. I have noticed recently that a lot of acquaintances, when we are talking about stem cells, say, "Well, of course I'm pro-choice," as if that

Dena S. Davis, "Stem Cells, Cloning, and Abortion: Making Careful Distinctions," *The American Journal of Bioethics*, vol. 2, winter 2002, pp. 47–49. Reproduced by permission of Taylor & Francis Group, LLC, http://www.taylorandfrancis.com.

settles the question of how they feel about stem cell research. But think about the most common reasons people give for being pro-choice: women have the right to decide what to do with their bodies; women can compete effectively in the workplace only if they can reliably control their fertility; only the individual woman can decide if she wants to be a parent; making abortion illegal risks women's lives; unwanted children are less likely to fare wall. All of these arguments are compatible with the belief that an embryo has some moral status, even quite weighty moral status, just not weighty enough to overbalance the woman's right to make that choice. Judith Jarvis Thompson (1971), in a famous and influential article, has shown that even imagining the embryo as having the same moral status as an adult human being, does not entail that a woman is required to function as that person's life support system for nine months. Thus, legally at least, Ronald Green(2002) is not correct when he says that if an embryo were regarded as a woman's moral equivalent from the point of fertilization, a woman's interests could be overridden if they clashed with the moral claims of the embryo or fetus. Laurence Tribe (1990) reminds us that

> There is . . . only one place in the law where a really significant and intimate sacrifice has been required of anyone in order to save another: the law of abortion. If you woke up with [Thomson's] hypothetical violinist attached to you, the law—and, probably, the views of morality held by most people—would permit you to free yourself of him. When the law prohibits a woman from freeing herself of the fetus that is inside her, the law appears to work a harsh discrimination against women *even if fetuses count as persons.*

Thus, even a woman who would never have an abortion herself can be pro-choice, supporting each woman's right to make that decision for herself. Tribe joins legal scholar Guido Calabresi in making the intriguing suggestion that the Supreme Court, when deciding *Roe v. Wade*, unnecessarily insulted people for whom fetal personhood is a bedrock of their faith. The Court could have said, "Even if the fetus *is* a person, the Constitution forbids compelling a woman to carry it for nine months and become a mother."

Benefits Outweigh Moral Claims

But when the embryo is *outside* the woman's body, frozen in a pipette somewhere, none of these arguments apply. A person could be firmly pro-choice, out of concern for women's liberty and well-being, and still oppose the destruction of extracorporeal embryos. At the same time, as we have seen in Congress, even some staunch pro-lifers have come out in favor of stem cell research, finding that the prospective benefits for people now struggling with diseases such as diabetes and multiple sclerosis, to name just a few, outweigh the moral claims of very early, unimplanted embryos that would, in most scenarios, be discarded. Thus, thinking clearly and well-about stem cell research requires us to give up slogans and knee-jerk reactions.

Some objections are based on ignorance, such as the notion that cloning will enable us to 'copy' 100 Hitlers or Mother Teresas.

On the other end of the spectrum, stem cell research calls up the specter of cloning, with all the visceral reactions that word engenders. It is true that Advanced Cell Technology, a Massachusetts biotech company, is trying to use "therapeutic cloning" to derive stem cells. The process, if perfected, would go something like this: Jane needs a new liver, but cadaveric livers are scarce and never perfectly matched. So, a scientist takes cells from Jane's cheek and inserts the DNA into a donor egg that has had the DNA sucked out of it. The egg is coaxed to divide and grow, and, when it is perhaps 32-cells old, it is destroyed. Stem cells are taken from it and are used to grow a new liver that will, of course, have Jane's genetic blueprint and which Jane's body will not reject. The basic technique, somatic cell nuclear transfer, is the same as the process used to create Dolly [the first cloned sheep].

What Cloning Is and Is Not

What are the reasons people commonly give for being opposed to cloning of humans? Some objections are based on ignorance, such as the notion that cloning will enable us to "copy" 100 Hitlers or Mother Teresas, full-blown adults with the personalities and characters of their models. (This is the false image of cloning depicted in popular films such as *The Sixth Day*.) However, as Leon Kass (1997) reminds us, "cloning is not Xeroxing." Here are some other, more thoughtful reasons: concern for children brought up in the "shadow" of the parent, dead sibling, or beloved relative from whom they were cloned; suspicion that parents who choose cloning will do so from narcissistic motives; fear that cloning children "to order" will result in thinking of children more as commodities and less as precious gifts. Kass again: "Through cloning, we can work our wants and wills on the very identity of our children, exercising control as never before." Finally, the huge number of miscarriages and malformed births necessary to produce one Dolly should tell us that we are a very long way from safely using cloning to reproduce human beings.

But when the issue at stake is *therapeutic* (rather than reproductive) cloning, none of these reasons applies. The embryos created through this process will be destroyed within the first few days of their creation in order to retrieve their stem cells to begin the process of producing a new organ. People who believe that the embryo from the moment of conception is fully protectable human life will probably find it consistent to oppose therapeutic cloning. Although these embryos are not conceived in the usual way, they do carry the full component of potential "humanhood." But for everyone else, it is difficult to see the objections to therapeutic cloning. Certainly the fears and concerns raised by reproductive cloning cannot reasonably be used to oppose therapeutic cloning.

Fetal Research Devalues Human Dignity

Thomas A. Shannon

Thomas A. Shannon is a professor of religion and social ethics at Worcester Polytechnic Institute in Massachusetts. He is the author of many articles and books on bioethics.

Over the last two decades scientific developments have been proceeding at a rapid pace. Nowhere has this been more true than in human genetics. One cannot pick up the daily paper or listen to a news show without hearing of yet another new discovery, development or application of a new procedure.

There are two main problems with this steady stream of information: The information itself is becoming more and more complex and the applications are predicted to be revolutionary. Frequently the research is only at the very beginning stages. Much of this research has an ethical dimension. In this *Update* we'll take a look at the field of stem-cell research. We'll explain what stem cells are and why there are ethical concerns.

Most Americans have had some sort of a biology course in high school; some have had a college-level course; but few have had specific courses in molecular genetics or bioengineering. Thus we may have some sort of general idea of the topic, but not grasp the real core issues. Several ethical issues were raised with the recent near-completion of the Human Genome Project (the project that identified and mapped the structure of human DNA)—privacy, potential disqualification for insurance, the possibility of predicting some aspects of one's health at birth, to name just a few. The technology goes

Thomas A. Shannon, "Stem-Cell Research: How Catholic Ethics Guide Us," www. AmericanCatholic.org, March 2006. Reproduced by permission.

forward, however, and often without sufficient breathing room to understand the technology, much less consider its implications.

This happened again with the debate over embryonic stem-cell research. Research on adult and embryonic stem cells of animals and humans has been going on for several years, and a national bioethics commission made some recommendations about this research. On August 9, 2001, President [George W.] Bush announced his decision to allow the federal government to provide funding for research on 64 lines of embryonic stem cells. These lines came from destroyed human embryos obtained from in vitro fertilization clinics. The president's decision caused an enormous debate in terms of both science and ethics. Many commentators, religious leaders, scientists and members of the public weighed in on various sides of the debate, and an advisory committee will now monitor the research. But what is the debate about?

Many argue that adult stem cells are where the resources for stem-cell research should be directed.

What Are Stem Cells, Anyway?

First, what are stem cells and why are they so important? Essentially, stem cells are cells that have the potential to become many different kinds of cells. They are the means by which cells in the body can be replenished. In the very early embryo these cells are *totipotent*—that is, they have the potency to become any kind of body cell. In adult stem cells, the cells are *pluripotent*—they have the capacity to become a variety of cells, but not all. Scientists hope to obtain lines of these embryonic stem cells—large numbers of them grown from a common source—and coax them into becoming specific kinds of cells.

For example, a biologist at my college recently succeeded in having blood cells from bone marrow grow into nerve cells. Other scientists have recently reported success in having embryonic stem cells grow into three different types of blood cells. The goal of this research is to use these stem cells to develop various tissues that can be used to repair damaged tissues in the body—heart tissue to repair damaged heart, nerve tissue to repair a damaged spinal column or reverse the effects of Alzheimer's disease. The research is very interesting, complex and promising.

Which Stem Cells?

Now let's look at a particular kind of ethical problem. Which stem cells should be used for research, adult or embryonic? Many have argued that adult stem cells are difficult to obtain, very hard to coax into developing into other tissues and, consequently, their use would involve much more time and money to obtain the desired results. Up until very recently, this was generally true.

Over the last few decades there has been a strong affirmation . . . that the human embryo is to be valued.

But now research has shown that adult stem cells can be isolated and developed. If this research continues to be successful, there may be no reason whatsoever to use embryonic stem cells, which requires destruction of early embryos and poses a serious ethical problem. Many argue that adult stem cells are where the resources for stem-cell research should be directed. Continued success in this area would essentially eliminate the need for embryonic stem cells—and put an end to a major ethical problem.

But the problem is that the Bush proposal—and indeed the desire of many scientists and many in Congress—is to use federal funds to support research on stem cells extracted from *already destroyed* human embryos. Is this ethical? There are actually two ethical questions here: First, is the destruction of the very early embryo immoral? Second, if a vaccine or tissue is generated from these human embryonic stem cells, would someone act unethically in using it?

'The federal government, for the first time in history, will support research that relies on the destruction of some defenseless human beings for the possible benefit to others.'

Over the last few decades there has been a strong affirmation by the pope and bishops that the human embryo is to be valued and, in effect, treated as a person from the time of fertilization forward. It is not to be destroyed or seen as disposable tissue that can be used in research as any other tissue might be. Nor should such embryos be generated specifically for research purposes. This of course is possible, given the technology of in vitro, "outside the body," fertilization. And in fact, one fertility clinic in Virginia has reported that in fact that is exactly what it is doing.

Reactions from Popes and Bishops

What is the moral status of the early embryo? Pope John Paul II gave his perspective on this debate in an address to President Bush on July 23, 2001, during his papal visit. The pope rearticulated his position on the use of embryos by saying: "Experience is already showing how a tragic coarsening of consciences accompanies the assault on innocent human life in the womb, leading to accommodation and acquiescence in the face of other related evils such as euthanasia, infanticide and, most recently, proposals for the creation for research purposes of human embryos, destined to be destroyed in the process." The pope also called for the United States to show the world that we can be masters and not products of technology.

In a similar, though more specific response to the Bush stem-cell proposal, Bishop Joseph A. Fiorenza, then president of the U.S. Conference of Catholic Bishops, said: "However, the trade-off [Bush] has announced is morally unacceptable: The federal government, for the first time in history, will support research that relies on the destruction of some defenseless human beings for the possible benefit to others. However such a decision is hedged about with qualification, it allows our nation's research enterprise to cultivate a disrespect for human life. . . . The President's policy may therefore prove to be as unworkable as it is morally wrong, ultimately serving only those whose goal is unlimited embryo research."

[The Catholic Church recognizes] that as a practical matter ensoulment is coincident with fertilization.

These claims are reflective of the traditional teaching recently restated, for example, in the Instruction from the Congregation for the Doctrine of the Faith, *Donum Vitae*, that the "human being is to be respected and treated as a person from the moment of conception and therefore from that same moment his rights as a person must be recognized."

The Instruction is careful to note that the Church has not taken a philosophical position on the time of ensoulment. However, "From the moment of conception, the life of every human being is to be respected in an absolute way . . ." (*Donum Vitae*, Introduction).

While the hierarchy of the Catholic Church has left open the resolution of the actual time of ensoulment, it has in fact insisted that the prudent response would be to recognize that as a practical matter ensoulment is coincident with fertilization. This position, combined with the traditional respect-for-life position of the Church, is what propels its opposition to embryonic stem-cell research.

The Beginning of Life

Some, while respecting this teaching of the Church, make further ethical observations about the early embryo. First, fertilization is a process that takes about 24 hours to complete and therefore is not a specific moment one can point to. As a side note, should a human be cloned, there would be no fertilization at all because the nucleus of one cell is placed into another cell that has its nucleus removed and is stimulated to begin cell division. The life of that individual would not begin at fertilization.

Second, the whole development of an embryo into a fetus and eventually into a child is a process, not a series of sharply defined steps. This is important because it is really difficult to tell precisely where a fetus is in the process of development. One knows where the fetus is after the stage has been entered into. It is not easy to make precise developmental statements and then moral judgments made in relation to them.

But more specifically, many ethicists focus on the fact that up until about a week or so into the pregnancy, the fertilized egg has the capacity to divide and become identical twins. In some cases it has been observed that such divided eggs blend back together into one blastocyst (what the fertilized egg is called at around 4–5 days of development).

And if the egg is fertilized in vitro, one cell can be removed (to have its genetic structure analyzed) and the developmental process is not harmed. In fact, all the cells of the blastocyst can be separated and each has the capacity to become a whole human being. This point is clearly important biologically: These cells can become either a whole organism or be coaxed into becoming any specialized cell in the body.

But this is important philosophically also. Because the cells of the blastocyst can be divided so that each part can become a whole, the blastocyst lacks true individuality—the capacity not to be able to be divided.

If one were to divide me, you would wind up with two halves. If one divides the cells of the blastocyst, one obtains several cells all capable of becoming individuals. The reason why this is philosophically important is that if the organism is not first an individual, it is difficult to understand how it could be a person. Being an individual organism is a first necessary, though certainly not sufficient, stage for being a person.

On the basis of the argument that the blastocyst is not yet an individual, some would argue that while the blastocyst is a living organism, possessing the human genetic code, such an organism is indeed valuable, but its value is not yet that accorded to a person.

The basis for rejecting such procedures is the recognition of the human embryo's being accepted as a full human person.

Therefore, some would conclude that killing the human blastocyst is not murder because there is as yet no personal subject to experience that wrong. Such a killing is a disvalue, to be sure, but a disvalue that might be offset by other positive values, such as health. The conclusion that some would draw, then, is that at least a case can be made for the use of human embryos in stem-cell research.

Once again, the Church does not endorse this view. The specific reason for the rejection of this position is the affirmation that fertilization, the time when egg and sperm merge and form a new genotype, is considered to be the biological beginning of the new human life. Together with this affirmation is the correlative presumption that this is the time of the infusion of the soul. Although there is no official doctrine on this position, the attitude of the Church is that moral priority should be given to this position.

The second problem is, could someone use a vaccine or tissues from such research in an ethical way? The term for this problem in moral theology is called *cooperation*. It can be either *formal* or *material*. Formal cooperation involves a person directly intending to participate in the evil act of another. For example, a person would be formally cooperating with a moral wrong if he or she obtained drugs and helped prepare them so they can be used for euthanasia.

Cooperation may be material, not formal, if a person does not intend the evil act but may be involved in some of its consequences. For example, a nurse who is opposed to abortion but works in a hospital where abortions are occasionally performed may still provide nursing care for the woman who came for abortion.

In the case of stem-cell research, this framework of degrees of cooperation allows several responses to be proposed. First, the patient need not intend the destruction of the embryos and thus any cooperation would not be formal. Thus, one could use the vaccines without an ethical breach. Second, the moral distance between the use of the vaccine by the patient and the original research is so great as to render any cooperation remote at best.

Finally, for use of the research to be immoral, the act of destroying a blastocyst must itself be immoral. If one follows the line of reasoning that the blastocyst is not yet an individual and, therefore, not yet a person, its killing would certainly be a disvalue but would not be a moral evil having the equivalence of murder. Thus individuals would be able to use the clinical products that come from such research.

Such reasoning would be unacceptable to the teaching of, for example, *Donum Vitae* or the encyclical letter of John Paul II, *Evangelium Vitae*. The basis for rejecting such procedures is the recognition of the human embryo's being accepted as a full human person from the moment of conception and, therefore, having an intrinsic dignity and value that cannot be compromised in the name of other values.

The Broader Ethical Question

But there is another question that is, I think, equally as important as the ethics of the use of human embryos in research. That question is a public policy question: Should we continue with our policy of research into high-tech, expensive therapies that may not be available to many citizens because they are uninsured, underinsured, or because their insurance plans might not cover experimental treatments? The dominant trend in American medicine is high-tech intervention to cure or try to maintain the status quo of a patient. The implantation of a new model of an artificial heart is another example of such high-tech intervention. Clearly many of these interventions do save lives. And significant developments have been made in the treatment of many forms of cancer. But some perceptions of the success of these interventions are inflated. One study showed that on television shows the success rate of cardiopulmonary resuscitation is over 70%. In real hospitals, however, the success rate is under 5%. This is not in itself a reason not to do CPR, but perhaps we might question whether it is appropriate in the particular circumstances of this patient.

The stem-cell debate might be an opportunity for us to ask if we should not, as a nation, begin to focus on prevention rather than cure as our dominant health-care strategy.

The stem-cell debate might be an opportunity for us to ask if we should not, as a nation, begin to focus on prevention rather than cure as our dominant health-care strategy.

Prevention will not prevent all diseases and will not help if there is a trauma such as a car accident. But a strategy of prevention including services such as care for pregnant women including proper diet information, well-baby exams including vaccinations, and information on lifestyle issues such as diet, smoking and excess drinking would go a long way to preventing the early onset of many diseases.

The resistance to removing or restricting the use of soda and candy machines in elementary and secondary schools shows that we have a long way to go in even thinking about the most elemental forms of prevention of disease.

Of course prevention is rather boring. It certainly would make for very dull TV shows. Who would not rather watch the fast-paced, high-tech ER than a physician instruct a person in a proper diet? Anyway, who wants to watch his or her diet all the time? Who has time for exercise and all the other things we learn are good for us? Prevention is a hard sell. But, in the long run, it is better to try to prevent heart disease than repair a damaged heart. It is better to manage one's diet than take insulin continuously or have a leg amputated because of circulation problems resulting from diabetes.

Spending Carefully

I am not arguing that we should abandon research or high-tech medicine. I am arguing that we as a country seriously need a national debate on health care and the kind of interventions that would be beneficial for all citizens, not just the wealthy.

Currently, it seems like much research on specific diseases is driven by powerful lobbying groups who have celebrity spokespersons who sometimes have the disease for which funding is sought. Parents whose children are afflicted with terrible diseases bring their children to congressional hearing rooms. The implication is that if Congress does not fund this particular legislation and a relative dies, it is the direct fault of Congress. But we know that we cannot fund research for all diseases, and certainly we cannot fund them equally. While all of us are sympathetic to the plight of the sick and suffering, a genuine ethical question is, who get access to such congressional hearings? One seldom sees the poor, the socially marginalized, the unemployed, the underinsured moving about in these circles. How does health-care policy affect their lives, particularly since they probably have no insurance to begin with?

What I am arguing here is that the stem-cell debate focuses our attention on yet another critical and important technical development in the fight against disease. Yet it also should make us question whether we as a country should channel all our resources to this form of research, or should we also begin to devote resources to prevention. Our health-care budget is limited; thus the question of the justice of how such resources are allocated is a critical one.

In addressing all of the questions covered in this *Update*, it's important to remember the Church does not wish merely to be a naysayer against development and scientific progress. In fact, the Church is very positive and supportive about advances in science that improve the quality of human life.

Most of the world knows that the Church works in many places, often in areas of high poverty, seeking to help liberate the human family from disease. In evaluating how to move ahead, whether it is in the laboratory or in society at large, always we are to remember an underlying principle: to value the dignity of human life.

New Scientific Breakthroughs Make Fetal Research Obsolete

Kathryn Jean Lopez and Robert P. George

Kathryn Jean Lopez is an editor with National Review Online; *Robert P. George is a member of the President's Council on Bioethics, a professor of Jurisprudence, and director of the James Madison Program in American Ideals and Institutions at Princeton University.*

In a recent [June 20, 2005,] *Wall Street Journal* opinion piece, Princeton's Robert P. George teamed up with Dr. Markus Grompe—"a professor of genetics at the Oregon Health and Science University, director of the Oregon Stem Cell Center and a member of the International Society for Stem Cell Research"—to herald the promise of an alternative to ethically challenged embryonic-stem-cell research.

NRO [National Review Online] Editor Kathryn Lopez recently asked George, a member of the President's Council on Bioethics, to talk a little about the future of stem-cell research and some of the heated rhetoric surrounding the issue.

NATIONAL REVIEW ONLINE: Last week [June 20, 2005,] in the *New York Times*, Mario Cuomo [former New York governor] wrote, "So far neither Mr. [George] Bush nor religious believers have convinced a majority of Americans that the use of embryonic stem cells inevitably entails the murder of a human being. Most Americans, vividly aware of the millions of tragic victims of Alzheimer's, Parkinson's, cancer and spinal cord injuries, believe that embryonic stem cell research may provide cures. They will demand that Congress act to realize that potential."

You must have been fuming.

ROBERT P. GEORGE: One really does wish that Governor Cuomo would defend his views with arguments. If he really thinks that human embryos are something other than human beings at the earliest stage of their natural development, he should state his reasons for believing such a thing. He should explain to us the basis of his judgment, if it is indeed his judgment, that every major text in the field of human embryology is simply in error on the point. After all, the question of whether a human embryo is or is not a whole living member of the species Homo sapiens is not one to be resolved in the mind of any conscientious citizen or morally serious policy maker by examining public-opinion polling data.

There is no mystery about when the life of a new human individual begins.

At the same time, it should be noted that Cuomo doesn't even manage to do justice to public-opinion polls on the question of embryo-killing. For what it is worth, polls stating the question in an unbiased fashion tend to show that a majority of Americans do not support the practice of destroying human embryos for biomedical research, and certainly oppose the *creation* of embryos by cloning for research—so-called "therapeutic cloning"—or any other purpose.

NRO: Is he just ignoring reality?

GEORGE: Yes. In dodging the moral argument against embryo killing, he is ignoring the basic facts of human embryology and developmental biology. There is no mystery about when the life of a new human individual begins. It is not a matter of subjective opinion or private religious belief. One finds the answer not by consulting one's viscera or searching through the Bible or the Koran; one finds it, rather, in the basic texts of the relevant scientific disciplines. Those texts are clear. Although none of us was ever a sperm cell or an ovum, each of us was, at an earlier stage of development, an embryo, just as each of us was an adolescent, a child, an infant, and a fetus. Each of us, by directing his own integral organic functioning, developed himself (sex is determined from the beginning) from the embryonic, into and through the fetal, infant, child, and adolescent stages, and into adulthood with his unity and determinateness intact. One's identity as a human being does not vary with or depend upon one's location, environment, age, size, stage of development, or condition of dependency.

There is another piece of reality that Cuomo is ignoring. He is imagining—or at least encouraging others to imagine— that embryo-destructive research holds the key to curing horrible diseases, such as Alzheimer's, Parkinson's, and cancer. The truth is that we do not know when, *or even whether,* embryonic stem cells will prove to be useful in treating *any* disease. . . .

There are people suffering from a variety of diseases who have been helped and even cured by adult-stem-cell therapies.

We cannot say with certainty that embryonic cells will never prove therapeutically useful in treating other diseases, but as a matter of sheer fact not a single embryonic-stem-cell therapy is even in clinical trials. No one knows how to prevent tumor formation and other problems arising from the use of embryonic stem cells. No one knows whether these problems will be solved or solved before other research strategies render embryonic research obsolete. Like [politicians] John Kerry, John Edwards, and Ron Reagan, Cuomo is elevating the hopes of suffering people and their families who are desperate for cures and eager to believe that if only embryonic-stem-cell research were federally funded they or their loved ones would be restored to health.

Indeed, Cuomo supposes that the American people are about to rise up and demand that the Congress open the money faucet. He imagines that the voting public will not tolerate politicians who stand their ground against the funding of embryo-destructive research. But, again, the former governor is disregarding reality....

NRO: Cuomo aside, is a silence starting to be broken about adult-stem-cell research and other alternatives to embryonic-stem-cell research?

GEORGE: Yes, the word is getting out about actual therapeutic breakthroughs using non-embryonic stem cells, such as cells harvested from umbilical cord blood, bone marrow, fat, and other sources. There are people suffering from a variety of diseases who have been helped and even cured by adult-stem-cell therapies. Many such therapies are well along in clinical trials. Word is also getting out about alternative methods of obtaining pluripotent (i.e., embryonic-type) stem cells. Even those of us who oppose embryo killing and reject the hype about possible embryonic-stem-cell therapies recognize that research involving pluripotent cells is desirable if the cells can be obtained without killing or harming human embryos or violating any other ethical norm....

NRO: What has been keeping the media from talking about these ethical alternatives?

GEORGE: Most people in the mainstream media favor embryonic-stem-cell research and have no objection to killing human embryos to obtain the cells. They are in the Cuomo camp. They view the opponents of embryo killing as "religious conservatives" and even "fundamentalists" who are trying to "impose their morality" on others and who are, in this case, trying to block advances in biomedical science. They think that talking about alternatives to embryo-killing (or successes with adult stem cells) only serves the interests of their political opponents. So many simply keep mum. There are, however, honorable exceptions. Neither Rick Weiss of the *Wash-*

ington Post nor Gareth Cook of the *Boston Globe* would appear on anybody's list of reporters secretly harboring sympathy for the pro-life cause. Yet both have published important, carefully researched stories telling the truth about possible alternatives to embryo-destructive research.

NRO: In layman's terms, what is OAR and what is the big deal about it?

GEORGE: Oocyte assisted reprogramming (OAR) is among the most exciting proposals for obtaining pluripotent stem cells without killing or harming human embryos. OAR is a variation of a broader concept known as "altered nuclear transfer." It combines basic cloning technology with epigenetic reprogramming.

I'll explain.

In cloning, the nucleus of a somatic cell (such as a skin cell) is transferred to an egg cell whose nucleus has been removed. An electrical stimulus is administered in a way that, if all goes as planned, triggers the development of a new and distinct organism, an embryo, that is virtually identical in its genetic constitution to the organism from which the somatic cell was taken. In OAR, however, the somatic-cell nucleus or the egg cytoplasm or both would first be altered before the nucleus is transferred. The modifications would change the expression of certain "master genes"—transcription factors that control expression of many other genes by switching them on or off. These genetic alterations would permit the egg to reprogram the somatic-cell nucleus directly to a pluripotent, but not a totipotent (i.e., embryonic) state. The altered expression of the powerful control gene would ensure that the characteristics of the newly produced cell are immediately different from, and incompatible with, those of an embryo. For optimal reprogramming, master genes known to control the pluripotency of embryonic stem cells would be used, for example the transcription factor known as "nanog." Thus, we would reasonably expect to obtain precisely the type of stem cells desired by advocates of embryonic stem-cell research, without ever creating or killing embryos. The cells used would not be embryos and would at no point go through an embryonic stage. Embryogenesis would never occur.

Don't trust claims about magic cures.

NRO: Is this in any way similar to Dr. Hurlbut's research? Is that something science should also be pursuing—with policy makers' backing?

GEORGE: William Hurlbut of Stanford University and the President's Council on Bioethics has been the leading voice urging scientists and policy makers to explore altered nuclear transfer as a possible method of obtaining pluripotent stem cells in an ethically unimpeachable manner. OAR represents a variation of Dr. Hurlbut's basic proposal. It emerged from discussions involving Dr. Markus Grompe of the Oregon Health and Science University, Dr. Maureen Condic of the University of Utah, and others. It represents an important step forward because it does not involve the production of non embryonic entities from which stem cells are harvested; rather, it employs techniques of epigenetic reprogramming of somatic cells to produce stem cells directly. Previously discussed versions of altered nuclear transfer left some pro-life advocates with concerns about whether we could really know whether altered nuclear transfer was producing truly non-embryonic entities as opposed to damaged or defective human embryos or human embryos pre-programmed for an early death (because, for example, they could not implant). OAR relieves that concern. Still, I and others advocating exploration of OAR want to begin with research using animal cells and proceed to the use of human cells only after OAR is proven to be technically feasible and ethically beyond reproach. We believe that this can be accomplished quickly and at modest cost. I certainly hope that policy makers will back this exploration.

NRO: When you advocate "creative science"—as you did in the headline of your recent *Wall Street Journal*—can't that get dangerous? I mean, we don't have a ban on a lot of stuff, especially when it comes to private research.

GEORGE: Science is a wonderful enterprise. It has served the cause of humanity in myriad ways. It has improved the average length and quality of our lives, and will continue to do so. Like countless others today, I'm a cancer survivor. Science made my survival possible. I can't begin to tell you how grateful I am for that. Yet, every sober person recognizes that great harm can also be done in the name of science and even in the cause of science. As in every other domain of life, in the sciences people can be tempted to do things that are morally wrong for the sake of what advocates of the wrongdoing will present as a "greater good." That kind of utilitarian thinking should always be resisted. Good ends do not justify bad means. The fact that a particular practice or strategy promises to advance scientific knowledge or even lead to cures for dreaded diseases cannot in itself justify otherwise unethical conduct. Even science is subject to moral norms. These norms—including above all the norm against killing innocent human beings at any stage or in any condition—place rational limits on what science may legitimately do. Killing, even in the cause of healing, compromises the moral foundations of biomedical sciences and cannot be justified. . . .

NRO: Most people's eyes glaze over when the topic of stem-cell research comes up. Are there just a few basic fundamentals people can grab onto that will serve them well in the midst of spin and worse?

GEORGE: Don't trust claims about magic cures.

Organizations to Contact

The editors have compiled the following list of organizations concerned with the issues debated in this book. The descriptions are derived from materials provided by the organizations. All have publications or information available for interested readers. The list was compiled on the date of publication of the present volume; names, addresses, and phone numbers may change. Be aware that many organizations take several weeks or longer to respond to inquiries, so allow as much time as possible.

ACLU Reproductive Freedom Project
125 Broad St., 17th Floor, New York, NY   10004
(212) 607-3300 • fax: (212) 607-3318
Web site: www.aclu.org/reproductiverights/index.html

A branch of the American Civil Liberties Union, the project coordinates efforts in litigation, advocacy, and public education to guarantee the constitutional right to reproductive choice. Its mission is to ensure that reproductive decisions will be informed, meaningful, and without hindrance or coercion from the government. The project disseminates fact sheets, pamphlets, and editorial articles and publishes the quarterly newsletter *Reproductive Rights Update*.

Advocates for Youth
2000 M St. NW, Suite 750, Washington, DC   20036
(202) 419-3420 • fax (202) 419-1448
Web site: www.advocatesforyouth.org/

Advocates for Youth is an educational organization dedicated to improving the quality of life for adolescents by reducing the incidence of sexually transmitted diseases and unwanted teenage pregnancies and by advocating minors' access to legal abortion. It opposes laws mandating parental consent or notification for a minor's abortion. The organization publishes educational guides and curricula, fact sheets, reports, and the quarterly newsletter *Transitions*.

Alan Guttmacher Institute (AGI)
120 Wall St., New York, NY   10005
(212) 248-1111 • fax: (212) 248-1951
e-mail: info@agi-usa.org
Web site: www.agi_usa.org

AGI works to safeguard the reproductive rights of women and men worldwide. The institute advocates the right to a safe and legal abortion and provides extensive statistical information on abortion.

American Life League (ALL)
PO Box 1350, Stafford, VA   22555
(540) 659-4171 • fax: (540) 659-2586
e-mail: JBrown@ALL.org
Web site: www.all.org/index.php

ALL is an organization of individuals opposed to abortion. Its primary goal is the passage of an amendment to the U.S. Constitution that would recognize the personhood of the unborn fetus and secure constitutional protection from the moment of fertilization. ALL monitors congressional activities dealing with pro-life issues and provides information on the physical and psychological risks of abortion. The league produces and publishes books, booklets, fact sheets, pamphlets, the biweekly newsletter *Communiqué*, the bimonthly magazine *Celebrate Life*, and the educational video series *Celebrate Life!*

Catholics for a Free Choice (CFFC)
1436 U St. NW, Suite 301, Washington, DC   20009-3997
(202) 986-6093 • fax: (202) 332-7995
e-mail: cfc@catholicsforchoice.org
Web site: www.catholicsforchoice.org

CFFC supports the right to a legal abortion. It promotes family planning to reduce the incidence of abortion and to increase women's choices in childbearing and child rearing.

Center for Bio-Ethics and Human Dignity (CBHD)
2065 Half Day Rd., Bannockburn, IL 60015
(847) 317-8180 • fax: (847) 317-8101
e-mail: cbhd@cbhd.org
Web site: www.cbhd.org

CBHD is an international educational center that examines bioethical issues from a Christian perspective. The center opposes abortion and genetic technologies such as fetal tissue research. It publishes topical articles, public testimonies, and the twice-yearly newsletter *Dignity.*

Center for Reproductive Law and Policy (CRLP)
120 Wall St., New York, NY 10005
(917) 637 3600 • fax: (917) 637-3666
e-mail: info@reprorights.org
Web site: www.crlp.org/

The center is an organization of reproductive rights attorneys and activists united to secure women's reproductive freedoms in the United States and around the world. It works as lead counsel in challenging restrictive abortion laws in several U.S. states and territories. CRLP publishes fact sheets, analyses, and the biweekly *Reproductive Freedom News.*

Feminist Majority Foundation (FMF)
1600 Wilson Blvd., Suite 801, Arlington, VA 22209
(403) 522-2214 • fax: (703) 522-2219
e-mail: femmaj@feminist.org
Web site: www.feminist.org

FMF advocates political, economic, and social equality for women. The foundation also strives to protect abortion rights for women. It hosts the National Clinic Defense Project and the Campaign for RU-486 and Contraceptive Research. FMF reports on feminist issues, including abortion, in its quarterly *Feminist Majority Report.*

Feminists for Life of America (FFLA)
P.O. Box 20685, Alexandria, VA   22320
(202) 737-3352
e-mail: info@feministsforlife.org
Web site: www.feministsforlife.org

FFLA is a grassroots, nonsectarian organization that works to achieve equality for women. It opposes abortion and infanticide, considering these acts to be inconsistent with the feminist principles of justice, nonviolence, and nondiscrimination. It publishes the quarterly journal, *American Feminist*, which includes such articles as "The Aftermath of Abortion."

Human Life International (HLI)
4 Family Life Lane, Front Royal, VA   22630
(540) 635-7884 • fax: (540) 622-6247
e-mail: hli@hli.org
Web site: www.hli.org

HLI is a pro-life family education and research organization that believes that the fetus is human from the moment of conception. It conducts an annual conference titled "Love, Life, and the Family" and distributes books, fact sheets, and the monthly newsletters *HLI Reports* and *Special Report.*

National Abortion Federation (NAF)
1755 Massachusetts Ave. NW, Suite 600
Washington, DC   20036
(202) 667-5881 • fax: (202) 667-5890
e-mail: naf@prochoice.org
Web site: www.prochoice.org/

The federation is a forum for providers of abortion services and others committed to making safe, legal abortions accessible to all women. It upgrades abortion services by providing them with standards and guidelines, and it serves as a clearinghouse of information on abortion services. NAF publishes fact sheets and bulletins, the booklet *Empowering Clinics: A*

User's Guide to Victim Impact Statutes, the semiannual *National Abortion Federation* newsletter, and the *Consumer's Guide to Abortion Services* (in English and Spanish).

National Abortion and Reproductive Rights Action League (NARAL)
1156 15th St. NW, Suite 700, Washington, DC   20005
(202) 973-3000 • fax: (202) 973-3096
Web site: www.naral.org

Since 1969, NARAL's mission has been to secure and protect a woman's right to safe, legal abortion. In addition to raising awareness about reproductive rights and lobbying for pro-choice legislation, the league also works to stop antiabortion violence, ensure access to abortion, and prevent unplanned pregnancies.

National Coalition of Abortion Providers (NCAP)
1718 Connecticut Ave. NW, Suite 700
Washington, DC   20009
(202) 319-0055 • fax: (202) 785-3849
e-mail: info@ncap.com
Web site: www.ncap.com

NCAP is a pro-choice organization that represents the political interests of independent abortion providers nationwide. The coalition lobbies in Washington, D.C., for pro-choice, pro-provider policies. NCAP publishes the bimonthly newsletter *NCAP News*.

National Right to Life Committee (NRLC)
512 10th St. NW, Washington, DC   20004
(202) 626-8800
e-mail: nrlc@nrlc.org
Web site: www.nrlc.org

NRLC, with its affiliate state right-to-life groups, is one of the largest organizations that opposes abortion. The committee is active in advertising and campaigning against legislation that favors legalized abortion. It encourages ratification of a constitutional amendment granting embryos and fetuses the same right to life as living persons, and it advocates alternatives to abortion, such as adoption. NRLC publishes the book *School-Based Clinics—The Abortion Connection* and the biweekly tabloid *National Right to Life News*.

Operation Rescue (OR)
P.O. Box 782888, Wichita, KS   67278-2888
(316) 683-6790 • fax: (916) 244-2636
e-mail: info@operationrescue.org
Web site: www.operationrescue.org/index.php

OR has been one of the most prominent organizations conducting abortion clinic demonstrations in attempts at reducing the incidence of abortion. Targeting clinics in large cities, Operation Rescue's tactics were threatened in 1994 when the U.S. Supreme Court ruled that abortion clinics could sue demonstrators. A law passed later that year also made obstructing access to clinics a federal crime. OR publishes the quarterly *Operation Rescue National Newsletter*.

Planned Parenthood Federation of America (PPFA)
434 W 33rd St., New York, NY   10001
(212) 541-7800 • fax: (212) 245-1845

PPFA is a national organization that supports people's right to make their own reproductive decisions without governmental interference. It provides contraceptive counseling and services at clinics located throughout the United States. Among its extensive publications are the pamphlets *Abortions: Questions and Answers, Five Ways to Prevent Abortion,* and *Nine Reasons Why Abortions Are Legal*.

Pro-Life Action League (PLAL)
6160 N. Cicero Ave., Suite 600, Chicago, IL   60646
(312) 777-2900 • fax: (312) 777-3061
e-mail: info@prolifeaction.org
Web site: www.prolifeaction.org

PLAL is a pro-life organization dedicated to ending abortion. The league consists of doctors, lawyers, business leaders, and other individuals who oppose abortion. It conducts demonstrations against abortion clinics and other agencies involved with abortion. It produces and publishes videotapes and brochures, the book *Closed: 99 Ways to Stop Abortion*, and the *Pro-Life Action News*, a quarterly newsletter.

Religious Coalition for Reproductive Choice (RCRC)
1025 Vermont Ave. NW, Suite 1130, Washington, DC   20005
(202) 628-7700 • fax: (202) 628-7716
e-mail: info@rcrc.org
Web site: www.rcrc.org

RCRC is an organization of more than thirty Christian, Jewish, and other religious groups committed to enabling individuals to make decisions concerning abortion in accordance with their conscience. It educates policy makers and the public about the diversity of religious perspectives on abortion. RCRC publishes booklets, an educational essay series, and the quarterly *Religious Coalition for Reproductive Choice Newsletter*.

Bibliography

Books

Randy Alcorn	*Why Pro-life? Caring for the Unborn and their Mothers.* Sisters, OR: Multnomah, 2004.
Jack M. Balkin, ed.	*What* Roe v. Wade *Should Have Said: The Nation's Top Legal Experts Rewrite America's Most Controversial Decision.* New York: New York University Press, 2005.
Michael Bellomo	*The Stem Cell Divide: The Facts, the Fiction, and the Fear Driving the Greatest Scientific, Political, and Religious Debate of Our Time.* New York: American Management Association, 2006.
David Boonin	*A Defense of Abortion.* New York: Cambridge University Press, 2003.
Gene Burns	*The Moral Veto: Framing Contraception, Abortion, and Cultural Pluralism in the United States.* New York: Cambridge University Press, 2005.
Christina Ryan Claypool	*Forgiven: Finding Peace in the Aftermath of Abortion.* Sherwood Park, AB, Canada: New Creation Ministries, 2004.

Stephen Coleman   *The Ethics of Artificial Uteruses: Implications for Reproduction and Abor-
tion.* Burlington, VT: Ashgate, 2004.

Raymond   *Anti-Abortionist at Large: How to Ar-
Dennehy   gue Abortion Intelligently and Live to
Tell about It.* Victoria, BC, Canada:
Trafford Publishing, 2002.

J. Butler Douglas   *Abortion Reproduction and the Internet: It's There, but Where?* Westmin-
ster, MD: J. Butler Douglas, Inc.,
2003.

Anibal Faúndes   *The Human Drama of Abortion: Seek-
and José   ing a Global Consensus.* Nashville,
Barzelatto   TN: Vanderbilt University Press 2006.

N.E.H. Hull,   *The Abortion Rights Controversy in
William James   America: A Legal Reader.* Chapel Hill:
Hoffer, and Peter   University of North Carolina Press,
Charles Hoffer,   2004.
eds.

Krista Jacob, ed.   *Abortion Under Attack: Women on the
Challenges Facing Choice.* Emeryville,
CA: Seal Press, 2006.

George F.   *Abortion from the Religious and Moral
Johnston   Perspective: An Annotated Bibliography.* Westport, CT: Praeger, 2003.

Scott Klusendorf   *Pro-Life 101: A Step-by-Step Guide to
Making Your Case Persuasively.* Signal
Hill, CA: Stand to Reason Press,
2002.

Nancy Levit and   *Feminist Legal Theory: A Primer.* New
Robert R.M.   York: New York University Press,
Verchick   2006.

185

Daniel C. Maguire, ed.	*Sacred Rights: The Case for Contraception and Abortion in World Religions.* New York: Oxford University Press, 2003.
Gregory E. Pence	*Classic Cases in Medical Ethics. Accounts of Cases That Have Shaped Medical Ethics, with Philosophical, Legal, and Historical Backgrounds.* Boston: McGraw-Hill, 2004.
Steven Pinker	*The Blank Slate: The Modern Denial of Human Nature.* New York: Viking, 2002.
Lorayne Ray	*What I Told My Daughters About Abortion.* Van Nuys, CA: Enlightened Press, 2003.
Michael Ruse and Christopher A. Pynes, eds.	*The Stem Cell Controversy: Debating the Issues.* Amherst, NY: Prometheus Books, 2003.
Alexander Sanger	*Beyond Choice: Reproductive Freedom in the 21⁰ Century.* New York: Public Affairs, 2004.
Johanna Schoen	*Choice and Coercion: Birth Control, Sterilization, and Abortion in Public Health and Welfare.* Chapel Hill: University of North Carolina Press, 2005.
Laurie Shrage	*Abortion and Social Responsibility: Depolarizing the Debate.* New York: Oxford University Press, 2003.

Rickie Solinger   *Pregnancy and Power: A Short History of Reproductive Politics in America.* New York: New York University Press, 2005.

Brendan Sweetman   *Why Politics Needs Religion: The Place of Religious Arguments in the Public Square.* Downers Grove, IL: InterVarsity Press, 2006.

Brent Waters and Ronald Cole-Turner, eds.   *God and the Embryo: Religious Voices on Stem Cells and Cloning.* Washington, DC: Georgetown University Press, 2003.

Periodicals

Debra Bendis   "Further Along," *Christian Century*, January 24, 2006.

Wendy Chavkin   "Chipping away at Roe," *Nation*, June 30, 2003.

Frederick Clarkson   "The Quiet Fall of an American Terrorist," *Salon*, December 10, 2003.

Francine Coeytaux, Kirsten Moore, and Lillian Gelberg   "Convincing New Providers to Offer Medical Abortion: What Will It Take?" *Perspectives on Sexual and Reproductive Health*, January–February 2003.

Jodi Enda   "The Women's View," *American Prospect*, April 1, 2005.

Amanda Gardner   "Amniotic Stem Cells Offer Hope against Congenital Heart Defects," *Washington Post*, November 14, 2006.

Alison George   "Teenagers Special: Going All the Way," *New Scientist*, March 5, 2005.

Michelle   "Laying Siege to the Last Abortion
Goldberg   Clinic in Mississippi," *Public Eye Magazine*, Fall 2006.

Cynthia Gorney   "Gambling with Abortion," *Harper's Magazine*, November 2004.

Jack Hitt   "Pro-Life Nation," *New York Times*, April 9, 2006.

Rajesh Jain   "A Practical Perspective on Abortion," *University Wire*, January 26, 2006.

William F. Jasper   "Advancing on the Pro-Life Front: Pro-Life Marches on the 33rd Anniversary of *Roe v. Wade* Underscore the Momentum Shift That Has Taken Place Against Abortion," *New American*, February 20, 2006.

John F.   "Abortion, Faith and Policies,"
Kavanaugh   *America*, February 16, 2004.

James P. Kelly   "Stem Cell Politics: Divide and Conquer," *Human Events*, September 5, 2006.

Martha Mendoza   "Between a Woman and Her Doctor," *Ms. Magazine*, Summer 2004.

Dennis O'Brien   "No to Abortion: Posture, Not Policy," *America*, May 30, 2005.

Ted Olsen   "Pro-Abortion Madness," *Christianity Today*, September 1, 2004

Leonard Peikoff	"Abortion Rights Are Pro-Life," *Capitalism Magazine*, January 23, 2003.
Katha Pollitt	"Feminists for (Fetal) Life," *Nation*, August 29, 2005.
Eyal Press	"My Father's Abortion War," *New York Times*, January 22, 2006.
Janet P. Realini	"Teenage Pregnancy Prevention: What Can We Do?" *American Family Physician*, October 15, 2004.
Mary Ellen Schneider	"Study: Parental Notification Laws May Lead to More Teen Pregnancies," *OB/GYN News*, February 15, 2005.
Karen Tumulty	"Where the Real Action Is ... for All the Debate in Washington, the Battle over Abortion Is Actually in the States, Which Are Imposing More Limits Than Ever. Missouri Is a Case Study," *Time*, January 30, 2006.
Tara J. Vasby	"Honest Conversations About Abortion," *Progressive*, June 1, 2005.
Lynn Vincent	"A Child Without a Choice," *World Magazine*, August 26, 2006.
Barny Yeoman	"The Scientist Who Hated Abortion," *Discover*, February 2003.
Michael Young	"What's Wrong with Abstinence Education?" *American Journal of Health Studies*, June 22, 2004.

Index

A

Abaluck, Jason, 99
Aborted fetuses, used in research, 145–146
Abortion
  aftereffects of, 80–81
  in the Bible, 43–49
  birth control as, 110–114
  central issues in debate over, 19–23
  complications from, 17, 47, 79–80
  in different stages, 39
  does no harm, 40–41
  economics of, 31–32
  essential nature of, 37–39
  as evil, 16
  funding of, 55, 63, 140–142
  good generated by, 41–42
  history of, 58–62
  illegal, 47, 51, 59–60, 106–107
  is not immoral, 34–42
  is a social failure, 78–81
  legal status of, 42
  reduction of, 52–53, 106–109
  selective, is immoral, 25–28
  statistics on, 115
  See also Access to abortion; Partial-birth abortions
Abortion clinics
  harassment of patients at, 132–135
  legislation aimed at closing, 86–87
  protection zones around, 133–135
  protests at, 15–16, 55, 76, 85–86, 119–125

  scarcity of, 56–57, 83, 90
  See also Abortion providers
Abortion counseling, gags on, 93–94
Abortion laws
  federal, 93–95
  proposed, 63–66
  recent rulings on, 74–77
  restrictive, 15, 52, 54–55, 99–105
  state-level, 63–66, 84–88, 95–98
Abortion protesters
  harass patients, 132–135
  murder by, is justifiable, 126–131
  Supreme Court ruling on, 119–125
Abortion providers
  killing of, is justifiable, 126–131
  scarcity of, 52, 55, 90
  should be protected, 136–143
Abortion restrictions
  Americans support, 68–77, 104
  are cruel and ineffective, 106–107
  are step toward abortion ban, 104–105
  on late-term abortions, 99–105
  See also Abortion laws
Abortion rights
  legal threats to, 15, 56–67
  reproductive responsibility and, 62
Abortion rights advocates. *See* Pro-choice advocates

190